A FEW WOI

BECOMING
HOLY
WHOLE
&
FIT

A 120 Day Devotional for Spirit, Soul, and Body
From the Hearts of Fifteen Extraordinary Women

Copyright © 2018 by FEW International Publications

All rights reserved. No part of this book may be reproduced or transmitted in any form or by any means, electronic or mechanical, including: photocopying, recording, or by any information storage and retrieval system, without permission in writing from the copyright owner.

This work is based on the experiences of individuals. Every effort has been made to ensure the accuracy of the content.

Quantity order requests can be emailed to:
Kimberly@TheFewWomen.com

A FEW Words On... Becoming Holy, Whole, & Fit
Publishing Coordinators: Kimberly Joy Krueger and Tamara Fink

Volume 1 of the "A FEW Words" Series from FEW International Publications

Contributing Authors: Kimberly Joy Krueger, Tamara Fink, Marlene Dawson, Susan Brozek, Kathy Thorsen, Kathy Carter, Margaret Bentham-Moe, Candice Moe, Rebecca Grambort, Luanne Nelson, Teresa Kliner, Tracy Boden Hennes, Jane Guffy, Danelle Sayler Skinner, Lisa Danegelis

Contributing Editor and Interior Layout Design: Reji Laberje, Bucket List To Bookshelf, www.bucketlisttobookshelf.com, reji.laberje@gmail.com
Cover Design and Interior Layout Graphic Elements: Mike Nicloy, Nico 11 Publishing & Design, www.nico11publishing.com, mike@nico11publishing.com
Author Photos and Marketing and Publicity Footage: Kimberly Laberge, labergekimberly.wixsite.com/thedramaden, Laberge.kimberly@gmail.com; additional photos contributed by authors
Publicity: Kimberly Joy Krueger, Tamara Fink, Reji Laberje, Contributing Authors

Scriptures taken from The Amplified Bible of 2015 (AMP) Copyright © 2015 by The Lockman Foundation, La Habra, CA 90631. Used with permission. All rights reserved.

The Christian Standard Bible. Copyright © 2017 by Holman Bible Publishers. Used by permission. Christian Standard Bible®, and CSB® are federally registered trademarks of Holman Bible Publishers, all rights reserved.

Scriptures taken from The Easy-to-Read Version (ERV). Copyright © 2006 by Bible League International. Used with permission. All rights reserved.

Scriptures taken from The ESV® Bible (The Holy Bible, English Standard Version®). ESV® Text Edition: 2016. Copyright © 2001 by Crossway, a publishing ministry of Good News Publishers. Used with permission. All rights reserved.

Scriptures taken from *The Holy Bible: International Standard Version*. Release 2.0, Build 2015.02.09. Copyright © 1995-2014 by ISV Foundation. ALL RIGHTS RESERVED INTERNATIONALLY. Used by permission of Davidson Press, LLC.

Scriptures taken from *The Holy Bible* King James Version are in the public domain.

Scriptures taken from The Message. Copyright © 1993, 1994, 1995, 1996, 2000, 2001, 2002. Used by permission of NavPress Publishing Group.

Scripture texts, prefaces, introductions, footnotes and cross references used in this work are taken, in part, from the New American Bible, revised edition © 2010, 1991, 1986, 1970 Confraternity of Christian Doctrine, Inc., Washington, DC All Rights Reserved. Used with permission.

Holy Bible, New International Version, copyright © 1973, 1978, 1984, and 2011 by Biblica, Inc.® Used by permission. All rights reserved worldwide.

Scripture quotations are taken from The Holy Bible, New Living Translation, copyright © 1996, 2004, 2015 by Tyndale House Foundation. Used by permission of Tyndale House Publishers, Inc., Carol Stream, Illinois 60188. All rights reserved.

Scriptures taken from The New King James Version®. Copyright © 1982 by Thomas Nelson. Used with permission. All rights reserved.

Scripture quotations are from the New Revised Standard Version Bible, copyright © 1989 the Division of Christian Education of the National Council of the Churches of Christ in the United States of America. Used by permission. All rights reserved.

The Passion Translation®. Copyright © 2017 by BroadStreet Publishing® Group, LLC. Used by permission. All rights reserved. thePassionTranslation.com

All remaining scriptures taken from www.biblegateway.com. © 1995-2017, The Zondervan Corporation. All Rights Reserved.

ISBN-13: 978-1987483918
ISBN-10: 198748391X

Categories:
Religion & Spirituality/Christian Books & Bibles/Literature & Fiction/Collections & Anthologies
Religion & Spirituality/Christian Books & Bibles/Christian Living/Devotionals
Religion & Spirituality/Christian Books & Bibles/Worship & Devotion/Meditations

FEW International Publications
An Extraordinary Publishing Experience

I believe women were created to be an answer for the problems our world faces today. The Fellowship of Extraordinary Women (FEW) was born out of that belief and today, FEW empowers women from all over the globe to live extraordinary lives and tell their stories.

FEW Monthly Meetings develop women's understanding of their true identity in Christ and empower them to embrace their God-given destiny. When I see women begin to understand that she was created to be an answer, she cannot help but to make a significant difference in the lives around her!

FEW's Certified Women's Leadership Course (CWLC) for Christian women changes the way they see God, themselves, and others. It catapults women into their God-given destiny as leaders on the seven mountains of cultural influence. I've experienced CWLC giving women unbridled confidence to be who God made them to be!

FEW International Publications, a #1 Bestselling Publisher with a unique writer-coaching model, is an extraordinary publishing experience. It is for women authors at all levels who are seeking more from telling their stories than just a printed project. I am privileged to watch authors connect, learn, and grow through the creation of a written work that impacts others and glorifies God.

Be Extraordinary!
Kimberly

Extraordinary Women; Extraordinary Stories
http://kimberlyjoykrueger.com/few.php

MORE FROM FEW INTERNATIONAL PUBLICATIONS

COMING IN 2018

Ladder of Hearts
*A Story For Parents
And Their Children*
By: Bestselling Author
Wendy Leppert

The Breakthrough Effect
The Third In Our "Effect" Series

A FEW Words Of Comfort For The Grieving
The Second In Our "A FEW Words" Series

"A Mama's Guide To A Grace-Filled Life"
By: Bestselling Author Wendy Leppert

THE STORY OF HOLY, WHOLE & FIT

"If you offered a retreat on how to be fit in spirit, soul and body, I'd be there in a heartbeat!" That was a comment one woman posted on one of my (Kimberly Krueger's) Facebook posts—and that is how the theme of *Holy, Whole, and Fit* was born. The idea thrilled me, as I've been on just such a journey for several years. I prayed about a retreat on this theme and searched the Word for a scripture that captured God's heart for His daughters to be *Holy, Whole, and Fit* in spirit, soul, and body.

The Lord led me to 1 Thessalonians 5:23-24 in The Message Version:

"May God himself, the God who makes everything holy and whole, make you holy and whole, put you together—spirit, soul, and body—and keep you fit for the coming of our Master, Jesus Christ. The One who called you is completely dependable. If he said it, he'll do it!"

I was so moved by this promise! Particularly the part that says, *"The One who called you is completely dependable. If he said it, he'll do it!"* Women need that hope! I need that hope! I went to work to make the retreat a reality and just six short weeks later, women came from all over the country to discover God's promise for them and to say "Yes!" to their journey of *becoming*.

At the same time, *FEW International Publications* was preparing to publish its first devotional by women, for women (although men may enjoy it, too). While on a road trip together, Tamara Fink and I were talking about that devotional and suddenly, she had an excellent idea for the topic! We should write the devotional on the topic of the upcoming retreat – becoming *Holy, Whole, and Fit*!

Tamara's idea was so divinely inspired, right down to dividing the book into four sections: *Nutrition, Exercise, Rest,* and *Water*. She reasoned that these four pillars of our physical health have clear and obvious spiritual counterparts and all are crucial to our health and growth as Christian women. By creating a devotional with promises from God's Word on the *Nutrition Of The Word, Exercising Our Faith, The Rest Of God*, and the *Water Of The Spirit*, as well as physical "Fit Tips" in each of these areas, we are, in fact, offering the perfect companion to women that are on their journey to becoming *Holy, Whole, and Fit* in spirit, soul, and body . . . and we are honored to do so!

Tamara and I would like to thank each one of the precious authors for pouring their hearts onto the pages of this beautiful devotional. Their stories and understanding of the scriptures is what makes up the substance of this book and will make the greatest impact on our readers. We are also so grateful for the love, support and encouragement they freely gave to us and each other throughout our journey together.

Very special thanks to Kathy Carter, Lisa Danegelis, Candice Moe, and Kathy Thorsen for contributing to our collection of "fit tips." Their passion for wellness is contagious! We are also so grateful to Tracy Hennes for sharing her gift and love for holy yoga with us in our very own session.

Our gratitude also goes to Kimberly Laberge for sharing her gifts and providing the beautiful photography and videography for this project. Special thanks also to Mike Nicloy for the beautiful cover and his patience with our process.

Last but not least, our deepest gratitude goes to Reji Laberje, for her brilliance, expertise and heart for each and every FEW Author. Reji's coaching, editing ,and gentle guidance are a huge part of the *FEW International Publications* experience and we are all so grateful for her!

Most of all, we wholeheartedly thank our God and perfect "Coach," Jesus Christ, for continuing to make us *Holy, Whole, and Fit* for the individual races He's called us to run. May we be found faithful as we cross our finish lines!

TABLE OF CONTENTS

Nutrition Of The Word	10
Exercise Your Faith	72
The Rest Of God	134
The Water Of The Spirit	196
Meet Our Authors	258
An Invitation To Become Holy, Whole, & Fit	264

"*A FEW Words On Becoming Holy, Whole, & Fit,*" the first release in FEW International Publication's line of devotionals, is more than a book to simply read.

- You'll be able to appreciate opportunities to journal with every single verse study by following prompts, or just by writing the thoughts that came to mind when absorbing God's Word.

- Practical fit tips are shared with each devotion.

- You can take in a section at a time, digging into the area where you need nourishment

- Choose to read from front to back, getting *Nourished by God's Word* to prepare you *for Exercising Your Faith*, which leads you to your need of the *Rest of God*, before getting refreshed by the *Water of the Spirit* to bring your learnings into the world!

- You could even share the book as part of a study with different facilitators for each of the four sections.

- Most FEW authors are available to present to your ministry, group, church, or organization. Like what you read? Consider inviting one of our authors to present a teaching on her devotion(s).

A FEW Words... MANY ways to use them on your own faith journey!

"May God himself, the God who makes everything holy and whole, make you holy and whole, put you together — spirit, soul, and body — and keep you fit for the coming of our Master, Jesus Christ. The One who called you is completely dependable. If he said it, he'll do it!"

~1 Thessalonians 5:23-24 (MSG)

Nutrition Of The Word

Have you ever noticed how sluggish or irritable you can get when your body is lacking good nutrition? Food is what fuels our bodies and if we're not putting the proper fuel in our body, it can become sick. You may be conscious of what you're putting into your body most of the time, but a simple vacation or schedule change can wreak havoc on your system! Your clothes seem to pinch, your energy plummets, and you think of napping all of the time. It's the same with our spirit man.

When we begin to get lax with our time in the Word, and "snack" on the ways of this world, we notice our spirit man gets weak and our soulish nature becomes irritable and sick. Instead of living the abundant life, we look for something to give us a quick fix or pick-me-up. It is in the midst of our search for spiritual snacks that we usually realize we are feeling the effects of our carelessness. Only then do we finally run to the comfort and security of our Savior's love found in His Word.

When we commit to a regular "diet" of God's Word, our attitudes and thoughts in our daily lives begin to come into alignment with His Spirit. The **Nutrition Of The Word** *of God strengthens our spiritual immune systems making it easier for us to resist the many temptations we face that lead to sin-sickness.*

When we meditate on His transformational Word, we begin to think His thoughts and—in turn—are more likely to do His will.

Our prayer for you, as you read these devotions, is that you will come to crave the nourishing Word of God above all else and choose to feast on it daily.

EAT WISDOM WITH THE FUTURE IN MIND

Rebecca Grambort

"If any of you lacks wisdom, you should ask God, who gives generously to all without finding fault, and it will be given to you."

~James 1:5 (NIV)

Did you know that wisdom means to be prudent or to think with the future in mind? I don't know about you, but many of my life choices have not been prudent. For most of my life, wisdom was something on which I came up a few sandwiches short of a picnic! As a distance runner, I do my best praying while I run. One day, while running, I was reflecting on a painful mess that I was in due to my lack of prudence. Admittedly, it would appear that I would continue to learn my wisdom through the consequences that followed my inability to think with the future in mind.

I ran as I cried out loud, "Lord, I don't want to learn my wisdom the hard way anymore! Your Word says that if any of us lacks wisdom, we can just ask for it and You will give it to us. Father, please lavish me with Your wisdom!"

As the Spirit guided me on my run that day, I felt Him spur me on to become a student of wisdom by digesting the book of Proverbs. It would be just the prescription I needed for my ongoing ailment. It was then that I realized that above all my other petitions, that I should make wisdom my number one request. I now see myself growing in wisdom daily as I pray, practice and digest the Word.

Are you making wisdom your number one request above all other petitions? You will see growing in wisdom daily as you pray, practice, and digest Word. Allow wisdom to help you hold your tongue, and become more patient, prudent, and self-controlled. With wisdom, you have a shield to protect your future.

Father, I am grateful that You are willing to freely give me wisdom when I ask. I don't want to learn wisdom the hard way anymore; but instead just ask You for it and digest Your Word so that it can protect my future!

Amen.

Nutrition Of The Word

When we eat, our choices affect our bodies. The same concept can apply when making other choices. Before making decisions, it's important to press pause and let wisdom interrupt the process. Wisdom asks questions that think with the future in mind. How will this choice impact the future? Who will it impact? Think of some decisions you need to make. Make a list of positives and negatives. How will these choices impact the future?

Nutrition Fit Tip:

Who needs store-bought salad dressings? Make your own base combining 1/2 cup olive oil, 5 Tablespoons vinegar or lemon juice, and a few tablespoons of water. Season as desired and use your imagination: toss with potato salads, warm it and drizzle over grilled fish or chicken, coat grilled vegetables, and—of course—use in your favorite salad!

No Leftovers From God

Jane Guffy

"And he was longing to be fed with the pods that the pigs ate, and no one gave him anything. But when he came to himself, he said, 'How many of my father's hired servants have more than enough bread, but I perish here with hunger!'"
~Luke 15:16-17 (ESV)

You have to be taught gratitude; you don't have to teach abundance.
The son's journey home was prompted by his absolute hunger.
God allowed his physical hunger to bring his spiritual needs into focus.

I take food for granted. I have access to endless kinds of food, restaurants, prepared foods, and stores. My kids used to complain about leftovers. I don't like them either. I eat when and what I please. I haven't experienced physical hunger like the prodigal son.

My stomach hasn't been empty . . . but my heart has been. Pride has no nutritional value. It will actually consume you from the inside out. The prodigal's self-inflicted poverty and hunger aren't much different than the empty condition that effects my life occasionally. Pride. He choked on and swallowed his pride - and he was still empty. Hunger brought his basic spiritual needs to the forefront. He pondered that his father's hired servants were fed more than enough. It sounds like there may have been leftovers. The son here would have coveted them. No one gave him anything - filling up on God has a self-serve quality to it. You have to accept the invitation and pull up a chair to the feast!

In our abundance of provision, we hopefully learn gratitude. In the prodigal son's lack of provision, he was brought to the end of himself.

Thankfully, most of us haven't experienced physical hunger to the point of wanting to consume the pods that pigs eat. We savor God's sweet grace and abundant provision, as the prodigal son came to the end of himself. God's patience, mercy, and love is constant, satiating, and will never leave us empty. We never get God's leftovers! We are served full portions from His endless buffet. God desires us to long for Him, feast on His word, and for Him to be our daily bread, to fill us and feed our spirits and hearts.

Thank you, Lord, that Your Word and the lessons of the prodigal son feed me. May I always hunger and thirst for the nourishment from your word. Grant me a tender heart for those who don't have the abundance that I enjoy.

Amen.

How are you filled when you sit with the Lord and feast in all His abundance? When you're fed with the Word to the point of (spiritual) leftovers, who do you share them with and how?

_____
_____
_____
_____
_____
_____
_____
_____
_____
_____
_____
_____
_____
_____
_____
_____
_____
_____
_____
_____
_____
_____

   Nutrition Fit Tip:

Eat smaller portions. Portion control is one of the best things you can do for your health—especially when you are eating an indulgence food.

THE SWEET NECTAR OF GOD

Marlene Dawson

"The law of the Lord is perfect, restoring the soul, the testimony of the Lord is sure, making wise the simple. The precepts of the Lord are pure, enlightening the eyes. The fear of the Lord is clean, enduring forever; the judgments of the Lord are true, they are righteous altogether. They are more desirable than gold, yes, than much fine gold; sweeter also than honey and the dripping of the honeycomb."

~Psalms 19:7-10 (NASB)

There are many health and wellness beliefs and programs all over the media these days. Since I struggle with weather related year-round asthma and allergies, I often look for nutritional ways to help me get outdoors. A friend informed me that honey is beneficial for allergies, so I decided to check out the health properties. I discovered honey counters pollen allergies, contains antibacterial and antioxidant components and boosts the immune system, among many other benefits. The best honey is locally harvested raw varieties.

Honey is mentioned numerous times throughout the Bible, but this mention in Psalm 19 intrigued me. Why does God mention honey alongside gold? We know gold gives us status in the world, but the purer gold lifts us up to the luxury seats.

Fresh pressed honey was considered a luxury item in Old Testament times, equal in status to the purest gold. We read in Psalms 19: 7-9 about the healing power of God's perfect law, and how it will positively impact our lives. Then, in verse 10, we learn the importance of feasting on God's Word. God is telling us He knows we all want gold, and we all want the best of the sweetest things He created. His greatest desire for us, however, is that we desire His best: a relationship with Him.

As we drink in the truths of God's provision for us, we can taste the sweetness of His love and mercy that have been pressed out for us through the sacrifice of Jesus. The revealed truth of God's ways is greater for us than the purest gold, and it quenches the spiritual taste of believers far more than the freshest nectar of the honeycomb.

Dear Lord, I have let things of this world distract me from You. I'm sorry. Will You please help me to redo my priority list, and place You on the top again? Thank You, Lord.

Amen.

Nutrition Of The Word

It is easy to get caught up in the days and trials of life. Think of a time when you allowed someone or something to take a higher priority than the Lord. How did the Lord show you what was going on? What did you do to get your priorities straight? How long did it take?

_____
_____
_____
_____
_____
_____
_____
_____
_____
_____
_____
_____
_____
_____
_____
_____
_____
_____
_____
_____

Nutrition Fit Tip:

If you have a sweet tooth, check out some of the low-carb chocolates on the market. Many companies now make products with stevia or other natural sweeteners. There are also recipes on the internet for making your own chocolate using unsweetened chocolate, coconut oil or cocoa butter, and stevia. Be creative!

Take Possession Of The Riches Of The Word

Kimberly Joy Krueger

"In the beginning was the Word, and the Word was with God, and the Word was God."

~John 1:1 (ESV)

"The Word became flesh and made his dwelling among us. We have seen his glory, the glory of the one and only Son, who came from the Father, full of grace and truth."

~John 1:14 (ESV)

I love biographies! When I homeschooled my kids, I became a biography junkie. We acquired many books about heroes of the faith as well as historical figures who changed the world—and I read them all. I just love reading people's stories! They encourage and compel me to live life with meaning! These books make an impact, to be sure, but no matter how well-written, they are just books about a person's life. They do not embody the life of the person they are written about! However, John 1:14 tells us that The Word of God is the embodiment of the person of Jesus Christ. The Bible is no more just a book than Jesus is just a man! Never before, or since, has there been a book that was alive with the character, heart, and life of the person the book was written about! The anointed Word of God is! It contains the heart, soul, and power of Jesus Christ—the power to teach, guide, change, save, strengthen, deliver, protect, transform, heal, and restore. It has the power to resurrect what's dead and recover what's been lost; just like Jesus. It holds the very power and provision that brought all things into existence in the beginning.

I heard a story about a family in Texas that lived in abject poverty. For years, this family struggled to make ends meet. Ultimately, they lost their struggle and their home. The new owners moved in, but they believed there was more to this homestead than the naked eye could see. They began to drill for oil and, in just a few days, they struck it! A fountain of oil came shooting out of the ground like it had no end! Although it was there all along, it did that poor family no good, whatsoever, because they had no idea what they had in their possession. Do we really know what we have in our possession when we hold God's Word in our hands? May we never stop drilling for the oil of the Spirit found in The Living Word of God which is the embodiment of Jesus Christ!

Father, thank You for Your living, active, anointed Word that bubbles over with life! May I embrace it, and believe it, and put its abundant provision to use in every circumstance I face! May I never live like a spiritual pauper again!

Amen.

Do you understand what you have in your possession in the Word or do you feel more like the poor family who was sitting right on top of their answer? Explain. How can you make the most of what the Word can do for you in your life right now?

___

Nutrition Fit Tip:

Drink a green smoothie every day with moringa oleifera, the most nutrient dense plant on the earth! Pack in more veggies by adding 1/2 an avocado and a carrot to your greens. Throw in some berries, flaxseed and protein powder for a meal that will keep you satiated and full of energy for hours!

DIGESTING WISDOM WILL PRESERVE YOU

Rebecca Grambort

"For wisdom will enter your heart, and knowledge will be pleasant to your soul. Discretion will protect you, and understanding will guard you. Wisdom will save you from the ways of wicked men, from men whose words are perverse...."

~Proverbs 2:10-12 (NIV)

One woman of the Bible who had experience with a wicked man was Abigail (1 Samuel 25). Abigail had to be wisdom; she was defined by it and she was unwavering from it. Danger loomed over Abigail's entire household because of her husband. Why? Because her husband, Nabal, had just insulted God's appointed anointed – King David! David's army lived peaceably alongside Nabal and even helped protect his sheep. But everything went sideways when David asked Nabal to share his food with his hungry troops. Nabal had the resources to help, but hurled insults at David instead. David was infuriated and would have killed every male in Nabal's household if Abigail would not have wisely intervened. She upheld righteousness, courageously overstepping Nabal's foolishness, and graciously fed David's men. She offered David an apology for her husband's indignacy and plead for his mercy. David admired Abigail's discretion and spared her family. In turn, David was also saved from his planned sinning of nearly annihilating Nabal's family.

Because of Abigail's wisdom, she knew when to act and when not to. She did not inappropriately submit to unrighteous behavior, but upheld God's righteousness. Can you imagine how fearful she was? Regardless, Abigail did not bow to fear. She bowed to her God, and appropriately submitted to Him instead of Nabal's unrighteous behavior. Her wisdom did what was right for everyone involved, protecting her and others. It even defended her character. Abigail's wisdom and discretion impacted many futures for good, because she allowed God's wisdom to permeate her soul.

Father, I invite wisdom to enter my heart. I know following Your ways will bring me peace and protection even when others choose to act foolishly.

Amen

Can you think of a time when other people's bad behavior infected you, like ingesting poison? God wants us to feed us good things that bring nutrition to our whole beings. In what ways can you partner with God to accomplish the goal of reaping the many benefits of ingesting wisdom and discretion?

___

 Nutrition Fit Tip:

A ten-day detox from sugar, artificial sweeteners, grains, dairy, gluten and chemical laden foods will reset your metabolism, cause you to lose weight and cleanse your body of harmful toxins.

THE LONG RACE

Luanne Nelson

"Thy word is a lamp unto my feet, and a light unto my path."
~Psalm 119:105 (NIV)

Sometimes, I just stand in awe at just how much He really does love you and me. Although, I still have to work at changing my old habits; I'm still a sinner. Dragging more of my truth into the light, I'll tell you I'm a recovering alcoholic for nearly twenty years now - a miracle story for a different day. Cigarettes are a thing of the past, too (*'Thank You, God'*). There's this nagging little eating disorder still surfacing from time-to-time and I have a temper that erupts like a mini-volcano every so often.

Every day I work on being better than yesterday. I'm a work-in-progress just like every one of His kids.

It took me a long time to realize He not only forgives us when we ask for forgiveness; He heals us and guides us back on track, straight back to His holy pathway - every single time we ask. He even hands us a lamp to light the way so we don't keep skinning our knees tripping in the dark. He improves and sustains us with His Word. What do you do to work on improving your spiritual life every day?

Physical light is the basis for all life on earth. So important is light, that God created light on the first day (Genesis 1:3). Without light, there would be no plants, no food, no way to find our way back to the path of his grace, forgiveness, and love. God's Word gives us direction in life; it nourishes us with the Truth and it lights up the path God wants us to be on.

Please light up my way, Lord Jesus God Almighty, nourish me and sustain me according to Your Word so I can continue to walk on Your path to holiness! Lead me to Your holy throne so I can crumple in a ball of thanksgiving at Your feet forever.
Amen.

Nutrition Of The Word

"Food for thought" is a common phrase. What foods are you nourishing your Spirit with daily? Carb up on His Word for the long race! Now is the time to become spiritually fit to make it to the finish line. What are you willing to do to run the possible best race toward eternal life? What is the ultimate prize you truly are seeking?

Nutrition Fit Tip:

Eat slowly. Put your fork down in between bites. It sounds simple, but so often we're all on auto-pilot and shoveling food in our mouths before our stomachs can figure out that we're full.

FEAST UPON HIM

Tamara Fink

> "'For the bread of God is that which comes down out of heaven, and gives life to the world.' Then they said to Him, 'Lord, always give us this bread.' Jesus said to them, 'I am the bread of life; he who comes to Me will not hunger, and he who believes in Me will never thirst.'"
>
> ~John 6:33-35 (NIV)

Bread is synonymous for food. What does food do for me? It nourishes me. It sustains me. It strengthens me. I've even used it to comfort me.

I always joke that Gary Chapman forgot my love language, feeding people, in his book, *The 5 Love Languages*. I find great joy in cooking for others. The only thing better than cooking for you is sitting around my table and eating it with you. We can laugh, cry or have deep conversation. It doesn't matter to me as long as I know I have made you feel special and cared for. Sometimes I fear food and I may have an unhealthy relationship, but—after reading this scripture—I see that my love language is the same as my Heavenly Father's.

God is our bread. He nourishes us. He sustains us. He strengthens us. And He certainly comforts us. Physical food leaves us wanting, but not God. He satisfies us completely. But just like I want to share in the meal that I prepared for you, so does He.

He left heaven to deliver his bread to us personally because it's His love language! He welcomes us into his family and offers us a seat at His table because He wants to laugh, cry and have deep conversations with us too. He desires nothing more than every time we think of food, we think of Him. His nourishment is the only one that will leave us full. It will complete us. It will leave us overflowing.

He surely answered the plea, "Lord, always give us this bread."

He never tires of us feasting upon Him; seeking His wisdom, His counsel, His provision, and His blessing. His desire is to be in an intimate relationship with us.

Lord, thank You for coming down from Heaven for me. Teach me to want you first and last. As I partake in my physical food, may it be a reminder that I need my spiritual food so much more. Nothing can sustain me or fulfill me like you can, Jesus. You truly are my bread of life.

Amen.

Nutrition Of The Word

When have you taken a bite of the Word that's left you wanting nothing more? What is your deepest longing? What is it that you need to God to fill in you?

_____
_____
_____
_____
_____
_____
_____
_____
_____
_____
_____
_____
_____
_____
_____
_____
_____
_____
_____
_____

Nutrition Fit Tip:

Make a nutrient dense breakfast hash by grating sweet potato and zucchini and sautéing it with minced onions and garlic for a few minutes. Adding a little nitrate-free bacon is also delicious! Serve as a base for fried or scrambled eggs. Make a big batch and freeze it in individual servings for a quick addition to any breakfast.

#PHYSICALLYFIT #EMOTIONALLYFIT #SPIRITUALLYFIT

Teresa Kliner

> "For the word of God is living and active, Sharper than any double-edged sword, it penetrates even to dividing soul and spirit, joints and marrow; it judges the thoughts and attitudes of the heart."
>
> ~Hebrews 4:12 (NIV)

I have been on a journey the last few years of becoming #physicallyfit #emotionallyfit #spirituallyfit. This has been my mantra. What I've come to realize is that—to have true health and be whole—we need health in all three areas.

My journey started with wanting to run a half marathon. During my training, I made a playlist for my runs. I started each run with the song *Nothing Is Impossible*. During each run, as I pushed myself to the limit physically I would recite God's Word over myself and push myself mentally past what I thought was possible. His Word and promises, spread throughout verses of songs, became what I was claiming for myself. This caused a reaction in me. It grew me emotionally and spiritually. It drove me to want to spend more time with God. Running became a time that God would speak to me and show me things in nature and relate them to my life.

What was going through my head...my thoughts...is what fed my feelings about myself. When I was pushing myself physically, and God was growing me spiritually, I learned to push myself in other areas of my life emotionally. I learned to believe in myself in all aspects of life, from fitness, to work, to personal connections. God grew me outside of my comfort zone. God works best outside of our comfort zones.

God's Word is amazing. It's not just some book. It's alive and active. If you feast on it daily, it will change your life. It will work its way through you physically, emotionally, and spiritually. It cuts through the shield we often hold up around others and reveals what's truly in our hearts. The more I listen and read the word, the more things are revealed to me...the things that need to be plucked and removed to make me "fit." The Lord isn't worried about our outer appearance...He's worried about our heart.

Lord You see my heart and You know everything in it. Reveal to me what needs to be changed. Use Your Word to fill me with Your power and to cut away unnecessary fat in my life.

Amen.

Our thoughts hold so much power in our lives. If we are feeding our thoughts the right thing we can be unstoppable. What are you feeding your mind? What area do you need to work on to be more disciplined? What's one thing you can do to start working on that today?

 Nutrition Fit Tip:

No pill, new diet, or new workout is the answer to your health and happiness. Stop looking for a trick; there are no tricks. You need to get real, get organized, and start working toward your goal if you want long-term success and happiness.

Worship With All That You Are

Tracy Hennes

"And you must love the Lord your God with all your heart, all your soul, all your mind, and all your strength."

~Mark 12:30 (NLT)

The cool morning air was being cut by the sharp rays of the hot summer sun, as I walked through the door to the gym. It felt great to be back after our family vacation. As I started the interval-training, a different feeling took over. Pain. My injury was worse than I had thought. I was forced to stop the exercises that I loved and had shaped my body since that spring. I was upset with myself, angry with my body, and questioning God.

Have you ever been frustrated by your own limitations?

In the weeks that followed and—in my search to not give up on physical exercise altogether—I found yoga. As I learned about yoga and practiced, I began loving it. I found myself in grateful prayer during yoga. Mark 12:30 carried me through that time. I was no longer frustrated or questioning God, but enjoying this new journey, and it didn't stop there. I sought out Christ-centered yoga certification programs. I dedicated months to becoming a certified yoga instructor; a Holy Yoga certified instructor! The time immersed in study, prayer, practice, and fellowship with people on a similar path, brought new appreciation for life and worshipping God with heart, soul, mind, and strength. I overcame the heartbreak of my injury, developed my relationship with Jesus, broke through a mental block, and continued to strengthen and shape my anatomy . . . my temple.

What an amazing gift!

As the Word of God nourishes all of us; heart, soul, mind, and strength, we should worship Him with all that we are. He wants nothing but the best for us in our entire being. If we find ourselves at a setback or limitation, don't give up, but seek new ways to love life and love Him. Take time daily in the Word of God for nourishment. When in a weak moment, perhaps Mark 12:30 could be our mantra?

Dear Heavenly Father, Thank You for giving us Your living Word to nourish every corner of who we are. Please help me, Lord, to worship You with my heart, soul, mind, and strength every day.

Amen.

Which of these: heart, soul, mind, and strength (body), do you find most difficult to love and incorporate into your expression of love for your Heavenly Father? Can you think of an appreciation for each (heart, soul, mind, and body), even in spite of possible frustrations or limitations? Enjoy living out Mark 12:30 . . . during what activity could you pray or meditate, today?

Nutrition Fit Tip:

Follow the 80/20 rule: Eat healthy 80% of the time. Indulge occasionally, but make sure most of your choices are healthy. Shop the perimeter of your grocery store where the food tends to be the healthiest and isn't primary packaged and processed.

HIS WORD IS A TENDER KISS

Kimberly Joy Krueger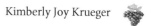

> "All Scripture is breathed out by God and profitable for teaching, for reproof, for correction, and for training in righteousness, that the man of God may be complete, equipped for every good work."
>
> ~2 Timothy 3:16-17 (ESV)

I was not a fan of this verse when I first read it. Being reproved, corrected, and trained sounded, well, unpleasant. I grew up feeling bad about myself, questioning my value, and knowing full well that I made a lot of dumb decisions. Condemnation was a close companion, so I didn't need any additional reminders that I was due for a swift kick in the you-know-where. (The fact that I was put off by this verse was evidence of exactly how much I needed the Word of God to do these very things in me, but I digress.) Thankfully, I eventually saw this verse through a different lens and it became a Word of Life to me.

Getting to know my Father's heart is what changed my lens and revealed that I was missing the point of this verse by a mile! The heart of this message is not that I am bad and need to be scolded. Instead, I see the love of my Father God, who embraces me as His beloved child and is at-the-ready to bring me up into maturity.

A baby enters this world without a clue and only learns and grows to the extent that her parents teach her. When she stumbles, while learning to walk, her parents do not berate her for it! No, falling is part of the growing up process. There is no condemnation; only love and patience while they teach. They even gently pick her up, kiss her tenderly, and smile from ear to ear, as they encourage her to try again. With that kind of loving guidance, correction, and training, in eighteen-or-so years, she will be all grown up—equipped for the real world—and ready to make her own mark.

So it is with God and us; He knew there would be many falls and much to learn before we would be *"equipped for every good work."* His Word is His tender kiss as He picks us up and waits with open arms and a delighted smile, as we try again.

Loving Father, teach, correct, and train me in Your gentle, patient Word, so that I may be complete in You and equipped for every good work You have prepared for me to do.

Amen.

What was your reaction the first time you read this verse? Why? When you fall, do you feel condemned or can you imagine your Loving Father picking you up, kissing you tenderly, and encouraging you to try again? Write down what you thought and felt when you watched your child or someone else's child fall. Do you imagine God feels any differently when you fall down? Why or why not?

_____
_____
_____
_____
_____
_____
_____
_____
_____
_____
_____
_____
_____
_____
_____
_____
_____
_____
_____
_____

Nutrition Fit Tip:

Don't DIET! Jumble the letters in the word and EDIT what you eat! It's very important that you track what you eat. If you don't know what you're eating, how can you change it? There are always patterns in eating; once you discover the patterns that aren't helping you reach your goals, it's much easier to change them.

How Do You Obtain The Fullness Of Life?

Candice Moe

"But the Fruit of the Spirit [the result of His Presence within us] is Love [unselfish concern for others], joy, [inner] peace, patience [not the ability to wait, but how we act while waiting], kindness, goodness, faithfulness, gentleness, self-control. Against such things there is no law."

~Galatians 5:22-23 (AMP)

Have peace and joy always seemed elusive? Perhaps tireless scouring has yielded nothing but façades. I've certainly been there. Many years were spent hunting down joy, laughter, and a sense of fulfillment. I assure you that your hunting ends in Jesus in choosing Him as Savior and Lord! As believers in Christ, we have the only ticket to the best seat in life, elevated beyond the cares of this world. Allow me to introduce you to your premium ticket: The Living Word of God.

To receive our Heavenly lot in this life we must submerge ourselves in the unshakable Word of God. It is in Him we draw strength, it's in His presence we are comforted, and it is in His arms we are renewed. We were created by the Father with a very unique design; His image and likeness. It stands to reason that proper functioning requires reading the manual and reading it often. I'd never enjoyed inner peace before journeying through scripture. The Bible isn't merely a book, *John 1:1-5, 14* says that *Jesus is the Word of God*, so every time you read the Bible you're literally ingesting Jesus Christ Himself. The Word is food to our spirits and direction for our souls. Abba's blueprints reveal that our spirit man must be fed a healthy diurnal diet of the Bible and prayer, to enable our souls' proper absorption of nutrients required for emotional wholesomeness. Our souls comprise our wills, minds, and emotions. Thus, a hearty intake of the Scriptures produces within us resultant choices, thoughts, and displays of emotions. Proverbs 4:20-22 inculcates that keeping the Word of God in our eyes and heart causes manifestations of physical health. Verse 23 goes on to admonish us to guard what we allow entrance into our souls, the very heart of our being, to ensure emotional stability.

Would you like love, joy, peace, self-control? I invite you to navigate through the scriptures, feasting on the Lord of Glory so the Holy Spirit can constantly bring out of you all that you consistently put in.

Father, thank You for Your Word and unwavering love. Illuminate the immense importance of reading Your Word. Give us Your Spirit of wisdom and revelation, let our hearts be knitted together with Yours, in Jesus' name.

Amen.

What are you consistently putting into your mind, heart, eyes and ears? What is being brought out of you? Write a prayer asking Abba to cleanse you and give you a new hunger for the nourishing Word, so that the fruit of the Spirit can be constantly brought out of you.

_____

_____

_____

_____

_____

_____

_____

_____

_____

_____

_____

_____

_____

_____

_____

_____

_____

_____

_____

_____

 Nutrition Fit Tip:

Discover what hunger cues your body gives you. Then wait for hunger to eat whole, clean foods that satiate!

WHAT DO YOU MAGNIFY?

Susan Brozek

"For You have magnified Your Word above all Your name."
~Psalm 138:2 (NKJV)

We've likely all heard the phrase that each of us is wired for worship and God deliberately designed us that way. All of us as human beings look for something to worship, to magnify. What do you magnify in your life? Do you magnify your successes? Your failures? Your achievements? Yourself? Your family? Your Creator God? If we don't worship God, we will find another, albeit very unworthy, object of our worship. We were created to worship God alone and magnify His beautiful name.

In the original Hebrew language, to magnify means "to promote, to make powerful, to praise, and to grow." When we are magnifying the name of God, we are giving Him His just reward—lifting up who He is. How do we know who He is? By spending time in His presence and spending time in His Word, the very Word that He tells us He magnifies above His name! *John 1:1* tells us, *"….the Word is God."* We can't ever fully know God's Name without knowing His Word.

The verse for this devotion has always touched a deep place in my heart and in my spirit-man, because, after all, God's Name is the Name above all names! And yet, He chooses to magnify His Word even above His own name:

> God is "El Elyon:" The Most High God.
> He is "El Olam:" The God of the Universe.
> He is "El De'Ot:" The God of Knowledge.
> He is "El HaNe'eman:" The Faithful God.
> He is "El Emet:" The God of Truth.
> He is "El HaGadol:" The Great God.
> He is "El Yeshuati:" The God of my Salvation.
> He is "El HaShamayim:" The God of the Heavens.
> He is "El HaKadosh:" The Holy God.
> He is the Great I AM . . . and "Ehyeh Asher Ehyeh" – the "I AM that I AM!"

Father God, how we thank You for Your Word and Your name. Help us to revere Your Word and increase within each of us a desire to know You in a more intimate way through Your Word and Your name. We magnify You this day, and we lift Your name on high. Receive our worship and praise, our worthy King.

Amen.

Spend a few minutes in prayer and ask God to search your heart for what it is you magnify in your life. Allow Him to speak to you as you ponder the importance of His Word over His very own name. Ask Him to speak to you about His nature, His character, and His attributes. Then spend some quality time in His Word.

_____
_____
_____
_____
_____
_____
_____
_____
_____
_____
_____
_____
_____
_____
_____
_____
_____
_____

Nutrition Fit Tip:

All carbohydrates are converted into sugar in the body. A diet high in sugar, elevates blood glucose, increases insulin resistance, inflammation and blood lipid levels, shrinks the memory center of the brain and promotes negative changes in our gut bacteria (responsible for regulating our immune system). Try swapping out regular pasta, rice, and potatoes for vegetable-based substitutes.

PURPOSE

Kathy Carter

"Do not be conformed to this age, but be transformed by the renewing of your mind, so that you may discern what is the good, pleasing, and perfect will of God."

~Romans 12:2 (CSB)

Oftentimes, we allow things of this world to define and place an identity on us; our home, car, weight, accomplishments. We are going along in life with all these wonderful fleeting fashions and life suddenly goes in a different direction. I informed my boyfriend of my inability to swim and then I proceeded to show him. Yep, he agreed! Little did I know, that was the beginning of a lifestyle that gave me purpose, defined who I was and made me feel very accomplished. From drowning rat to world championship Ironman finisher, that was me! So now what, twenty-five years later?

My Ironman days are behind me.

When it all ends, and life takes on a new adventure, it is not easy to redefine yourself. Oftentimes, you feel you are never enough. In fact, it can be years of self-doubt and insecurities, until you find that one thing that makes you feel important again.

Idolizing a lifestyle that is only temporary and allowing it to define you will only cause repeated hurt and suffering. Transforming your thoughts about who you are into how God sees you is forever freedom.

Romans 12:2 tells us to *"be transformed into His likeness who is inside of you and the pattern of all perfection."* Our maker created you and you get your value from Him. Transforming to this way of thinking will give you a true sense of peace and confidence. Do not let the world around you dictate the world inside of you. Let the world inside of you transform the world outside of you.

Dear God, Thank You for creating me into Your masterpiece that is perfect and beautiful. Help me to believe I am enough because You tell me I am. Help me to love me for who I am so I have enough to give others. I know I am a work-in-progress but I choose to believe You over all things. In Your name, Jesus Christ.

Amen.

How would you feel if you looked at yourself like God's masterpiece rather than defined as a specific role or within a specific lifestyle? What are some positive affirmations you can say to help you improve your self-image?

Nutrition Fit Tip:

Medium Chain Triglycerides (MCT) are an important type of fat for your body. Purchase MCT oil or oil powder for a clean and effective energy source. Add the powder to your coffee in place of creamer, or to a smoothie. Add the oil to salad dressings.

SATAN OPERATES IN DARKNESS; HE HOPES WE WILL, TOO

Danelle Skinner

"Well, no wonder! Even Satan can disguise himself to look like an angel of light!"

~2 Corinthians 11:14 (GNT)

Satan can disguise himself well, well enough to look like an angel of light, making it hard to identify him, let alone to be able to see where he is at work in our lives. This was true for me, until I started reading the word of God. The bible feeds me, nourishes my soul, and continues to teach me how to distinguish what is true, helping reveal Satan's attack on my life.

"But everything that is exposed to the light becomes visible...." (Ephesians 5:13 ISV)

"What is light? God is light." (1 John 1:5 NIV)

What do we have access to that is God? His Living Word, the Bible. Satan operates in darkness. He hopes we will, too, so that we will be stumbling around in the darkness. Unable to identify him and his deceptions. Satan is sneaky. That is why he is referred to as a wolf in sheep's clothing. His works are not bold-faced lies. That would make them too easily detectable. The light of God's word helps us to see clearly. It feeds us real, solid, and unwavering truth, making it possible to distinguish when something is fact or fiction, true or almost true. This way we can undoubtedly see when something is coming from Satan in disguise, rather than from the Lord our God. We must expose everything in our lives to the light of the Word, helping us detect the enemy and make his plots against us visible. This way we will know how to specifically pray against his advances on us to steal, kill and destroy. (From John 10:10 NIV)

Satan is not the only thing in disguise. Lots of worldly things are disguised as "truth" such as; money, the status of work, identity through worldly idols, and our numbers of Facebook likes. Nourish yourself with the truth of God's word, revealing His identity and will for you, so that you can guard yourself against the things of this world that are disguised as truth and look like an angel of light when they are not.

Dear God, thank You for Your living word. I am grateful we have access to a tool to distinguish what is true, exposing Satan in disguise. Please continue to help me to be able to identify Satan and his deceits and ploys against me.

Amen.

Nutrition Of The Word

God's Word exposes truth. Do you guard yourself with the truth of God's Word? If so, how? If not, I challenge you to start small. Commit yourself to reading one verse a day. Meditate on His words and let it nourish you with truth, opening your eyes to see the enemy clearly.

Nutrition Fit Tip:

Cook at home more. Portions served at restaurants are huge and you don't always know what they are putting into your food. Escape the hidden calories and make your own food at home from fresh ingredients.

Entrees For Living

Candice Moe

> "But solid food is for the [spiritually] mature, whose senses are trained by practice to distinguish between what is morally good and what is evil."
> ~Hebrews 5:14 (AMP)

Mature, responsible, adult, level-headed, reliable, dependable. Do you embody these attributes? Jesus' exorbitant dowry, secured Heaven as our home and Heaven Culture as our lifestyle. Salvation isn't the culmination but the commencement of fulfilling His mandate. *(John 14:11-13 AMP)* "Prepare ye the way of the Lord!" Have you embraced John's mantle? Jesus said, *"I tell you the Truth, unless a kernel of wheat is planted in the soil and dies, it remains alone. But its death will produce many new kernels—a plentiful harvest of new lives. Those who love their life in this world will lose it. Those who care nothing for their life in this world will keep it eternally."* Effective Christianity is reigning with Christ our King, where He's not only Savior but Lord. Lordship denotes rulership. Has Jesus been crowned atop your heart's throne?

Spiritual maturity requires surrendering to Abba's perfect will. Are you running to win? *Hebrews 10:14 (AMP)* says, *"For by one Sacrifice He has made perfect forever those who are being made Holy."* Our right-standing before The Father is His Gift, holiness is our choice and we're implored to choose it.

Spiritual maturity requires habitual one-on-one time with Jesus Christ in His Word, in prayer and thus, in His presence. At escalating junctures, it quite often entails setting aside things and foregoing old routines, that, while not necessarily sinful, could serve as impedimenta. Choosing activities that foster goodness and sacrificing those that may potentially lead away from righteousness are crucial.

"A little leaven leavens the whole lump." (Galations 5:9 AMP) *"Catch the foxes, the little foxes, before they ruin our vineyard in bloom."* (Song of Solomon 2:15 AMP) Ramparts are not only for your benefit, but also for those within your sphere of influence. Perhaps, you are the only bible someone may ever read. The Father loves you with great intensity. His plans concerning you are vast. Promotion hinges heavily upon development.

Daddy, in Jesus' Name, I request refinement and a willingness for growth and expansion. May Your glory reverberate from within me to a lost and dying world.

Amen.

Do you desire to grow up in Christ? To become spiritually mature, no longer needing milk, but able to digest the solid food of the Word? If so, what could be one or two "little foxes" or "leaven" that might be sneaking in and spoiling your growth? What solid foods from God's Word can you ingest so that you are growing in spiritual maturity rather than allowing God's vineyard in you fall to ruin?

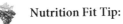 **Nutrition Fit Tip:**

Add antibiotic- and preservative-free Chorizo and Italian sausages to add zest and variety to many meals, while sticking with healthy proteins.

"What?!"

Luanne Nelson

"But He said, 'More than that, blessed are those who hear the word of God and keep it!'"

~Luke 11:28 (NKJV)

My ears don't work very well. I'm in the "severe to profound hearing loss" category on the audiology report I carry around with me. I have shown this paper sometimes to people to explain why I have a service dog in tow. Despite severely limited hearing, I'm able to carry conversations provided there's not a lot of background noise and I am wearing a hearing device in my left ear. A few weeks ago, I was chatting with a college roommate I've known for over forty years.

We were swapping stories about recent adventures when she quipped, "Luanne, you are an atheist magnet."

I thought about it for a moment. She's right. I am an atheist magnet. You see, non-believers in my life seem to want to keep one of their feet firmly wedged in my heart door. They challenge my faith, demanding proof. I serve up a steady diet of God's word mingled with my own experiences, putting it all on a plate of hope and faith mingled with love, patience, and a prayer. We both receive spiritual nourishment.

God uses all of us in unexpected ways. Every single one of God's creation has something to give to another human being, whether they believe it or not (Romans 8:28). When we cross that line and He actually starts using us effortlessly, it's not work, anymore. Even though my ears don't work, my heart listens attentively and hears the Word, loud and clear. It wasn't always like that, though. The more I read and share His word, the stronger I am.

How do you know you are truly hearing the Word of God?

God's Word is sturdy, steady, true, and life-changing. God gave us His Word to bless us. To listen means to "pay heed" - to have an attentive ear, to be quiet. To be blessed means to be "made holy" or "consecrated." To be truly blessed, we respond to the Word of God, keep it in our hearts, share it, and live it.

Father God, we ask You to open our ears to hear Your Word, to open our hearts to know it, to open our mouths to proclaim Your glory.

Amen.

Nutrition Of The Word

It's not enough to just hear words being spoken, any more than it's enough to look at food on a plate and not eat it. Think of ways you live out the Word of God after you've heard it. He gives us everything we need to run the great race - His Word, perfect spiritual shoes, and people who are hungry for His Word around us every day. How do you share His word with others?

Nutrition Fit Tip:

Eat alkaline-promoting foods. Research suggests that eating too many acidic foods can damage our lungs and kidneys. Balance out the acidity with foods that promote an alkaline body environment. Eat lots of root vegetables, cruciferous vegetables like: broccoli, cabbage, Brussel sprouts, leafy greens, garlic, cayenne peppers, and lemons and limes.

THE GOD OF THE JOURNEY

Susan Brozek

"Sanctify them by Your truth. Your Word is truth."

~John 17:17 (NKJV)

A lot of people are familiar with the oft-used phrase that "salvation happens in a moment, but sanctification happens over a lifetime." This is a very accurate characterization of the Christian walk. We receive Christ into our hearts when we call on His Name and receive Him as Savior and Lord, but the "sanctification" process (the process of learning what it means to be set apart for God and what that looks like as we live in today's world) is lifelong.

I have always said that God is a God of the journey, not just the destination. If we let Him, He has much to show us along our path to growth and mature in Christ. We need to keep in mind that we are essentially running a marathon, not a sprint! When we receive God's truth, by getting to know Him through prayer and His Word, and apply it to our daily lives, we begin to understand how the sanctification process works.

God's Word is truth, and it is His truth that sets us apart to live in this world, even though we aren't of this world. We are now part of God's Kingdom, but how do we live in this world while still staying true to God? It can be very challenging at times. Knowing the truths of who He is and who we are in His Word can help us tremendously. Also, keeping in mind that this world and the things of it will never be able to satisfy our deepest needs, gives us the perspective we need to seek God consistently for His sufficient grace.

The Greek word for truth is "aletheia," which means: not hidden, not concealed. The truth about God is available to all human beings, fully uncovered for us. Many people today talk frequently about "living their truths," as it pertains to their lives and specific situations.

The ultimate truth is found when we discover who we are in light of who God is in His Word.

Dear Heavenly Father, Your Word mentions that when we know the truth, it will set us free. Help me to know the truth of who You made me to be and how I can live Your truth in a way that honors Your name for all of my days.

Amen.

What have your expectations been as it comes to maturing in the Lord (the process of sanctification)? Many of us believe that we should be a lot further along in our walk with God than we are. But God would likely say that we are exactly where we are supposed to be. He meets us where we are and takes it from there. Describe some difficult areas that you know God is currently wanting to help you address in your life. Also, what is the most difficult aspect for you in terms of being in the world, but not of it?

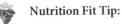 **Nutrition Fit Tip:**

"Low-fat" usually means high sugar! Check the sugar grams. Keep your sugar grams to under thirty each day to avoid weight gain and complications with your health.

SACRIFICE FOR YOUR SEAT AT THE TABLE

Kathy Thorsen

"He said to them, "I have eagerly desired to eat this Passover with you before I suffer; for I tell you, I will not eat it until it is fulfilled in the kingdom of God.' Then he took a cup, and after giving thanks he said, 'Take this and divide it among yourselves; for I tell you that from now on I will not drink of the fruit of the vine until the kingdom of God comes.' Then he took a loaf of bread, and when he had given thanks, he broke it and gave it to them, saying, 'This is my body, which is given for you. Do this in remembrance of me.' And he did the same with the cup after supper, saying, 'This cup that is poured out for you is the new covenant in my blood.'"

~Luke 22:15-20 (NRSVCE)

That which we cannot have, we desire even more. I experience this longing every time I fast for religious or health reasons. The most difficult restraint has been forgoing gluten, dairy, most grains and processed sugar indefinitely, due to intestinal permeability and an autoimmune disease. I have a deeply-rooted connection to these foods, as I grew up on a dairy farm and was responsible for baking a different dessert every day for a family of nine. During family and friend social gatherings, food is the centerpiece of the event and the thing around which we gather and relate. The feelings of disconnectedness and judgment when I'm not eating those foods, tear at my heart. My trivial discomforts, though, cannot compare to the suffering Jesus knew He was about to face as He shared the Passover feast with the disciples.

The body and blood generously given by Jesus established a new covenant making God's Kingdom accessible to all for eternity. Jesus had a deep connection to the food He distributed and desire to spend this time with His beloved friends for comfort to carry Him through His inevitable suffering. He came to the table with an eager hunger, not for the bread and wine, but for the desire to fulfill the prophesy that He was to die on a cross for the salvation for all generations to come. When we are called to give up our earthly desires, we unite that suffering with Jesus and satiate our hunger with the most fulfilling meal; the living body and blood of Christ. We, too, are invited to eagerly desire the nourishment for our souls provided through the bread and wine in the feast of the Eucharist. What could be more comforting or satisfying than to know that Jesus has made the ultimate sacrifice for the forgiveness of sins of all humankind and waits to share the Passover with us in heaven?

Dear Jesus, the words "Thank You," seem so trite to convey the gratitude I have for the sacrifice You made for humanity. Forgive me for the sins caused by my desire to be filled with earthly treats. I pray that I may eagerly attend the Eucharistic feast You have prepared so that I may be nourished by Your body and blood that will lead me to everlasting life.

Amen.

Do we hunger for more than food when we sit at the table with our families and friends? Is our desire to be obedient to God stronger than our inclination to eat and drink whatever we want? What do we need to sacrifice in our daily lives to be worthy to sit at table with Jesus?

 Nutrition Fit Tip:

Select healthier choices to have on standby in your fridge when hunger pains or emotional eating strikes, such as a bowl of fresh, cleaned, strawberries or blueberries.

BECAUSE I SHOULD

Tracy Hennes

"For I have told you often before, and I say it again with tears in my eyes, that there are many whose conduct shows they are really enemies of the cross of Christ. They are headed for destruction. Their god is their appetite, they brag about shameful things, and they think only about this life here on earth."

~Philippians 3:18-19 (NLT)

"Because I can." That's a recent ad campaign for one of the most popular drinks in America.

The ads feature a popular young actor talking of doing whatever makes you happy in life, regardless of what others think. The canned beverage itself, has no nutritional value, and in fact, contains at least two controversial ingredients that are suggested to pose health concerns and have been banned in other parts of the world. Just "Because I can," may not necessarily mean, "I should."

Imagine what our world would be like if we all took the "Because I can" attitude to heart in all of our decisions.

In Philippians 3:18-19, God pleads with us to not destroy ourselves with the preoccupation of our earthly appetites. If we focus on this life and what makes us feel good while we are here on earth, our motivation to satisfy that hunger becomes our top priority; an idol.

There is space within our heart that only God can fill. We may try to fill that space with a love of food, but instead of feeling satisfied, it will leave us looking for more. We will never feel absolutely complete without putting our relationship with God in its rightful place. If we spend too much time and energy chasing down false idols, whether it be food, material possessions, a relationship, career, acceptance, or achievements, we are not honoring the fact that Jesus died to save us from this very type of thing. Having false idols hurts God . . . because He doesn't want us to destroy ourselves!

If God were to come to you and, *'Why do you destroy yourself when I have all you need?'* what would you say to Him?

Dear Heavenly Father, thank You for wanting a relationship with me and for looking out for me. Please forgive me for the times I've put someone or something else before You. Help me, Lord, to seek my nourishment from Your Word.

Amen.

Nutrition Of The Word

In what ways does feeding the appetites of your flesh put you on a path of destruction? How are you emotionally impacted when you imagine God asking you why you fill the space meant for Him with other things? What can you do to ensure that your relationship with God takes the rightful place as priority for you?

Nutrition Fit Tip:

If you are avoiding grains but love granola, check out some delicious grain-free granola recipes. They are chock full of coconut, nuts, seeds and healthy fats such as coconut oil. Make and toss with plain full-fat Greek yogurt and antioxidant rich berries for a protein packed breakfast.

Rock-Solid Assuredness

Lisa Danegelis

> "For I know that my Redeemer lives, and He shall stand at last on the earth; and after my skin is destroyed, this I know, that in my flesh I shall see God."
> ~Job 19: 25-26 (NKJV)

I am often asked if I believe I am going to heal from the debilitating effects of psychiatric drugs. I always answer by saying, "I know I will." The words come without thought from somewhere deep within.

I was curious about my own answer, and looked up these definitions:

Believe (verb): to have confidence or faith in the truth, to give credence to
Know (verb): to perceive or understand as fact or truth; to apprehend clearly and with certainty

Believing is a strong presumption. Knowing is rock solid assuredness. This knowing is what keeps me staunchly moving forward on an agonizing journey that could otherwise lead down a deadly path.

Job's conviction in the above passage can be used as a concrete foundation for our own faith. In the earlier verses of chapter 19, Job all but curses God. He holds nothing back in his piercing tirade, even saying, *"My hope He has uprooted like a tree."*

Yet, in his very next breath, Job says he knows his redeemer lives and that he shall see God!

I think we can be quite sure that no one has suffered as deeply as Job. God made that clear by giving his story its own book. As he *"mourns in ashes scraping his wounds,"* after having lost his children and all he owned, he still does not curse God.

What a triumph! What a glorious representation of enduring faith tested by fire! Job knew God was faithful. He may have not known when or how his story on earth would end, but his eyes stayed on the prize: seeing God in eternity. The end to this epic story is well known; in his misery, Job even had the compassion to pray for his doubting friends and then God blessed him with a double portion of all he had lost!

Father, may my faith run deep, help me to know You as Job did!

Amen.

Read chapter 19 in Job. Think about the accusations Job made against God. Now focus on his ultimate surrender to God's sovereignty. Journal some of your own frustrations; don't be afraid, God can take it! Then surrender your frustrations at the foot of His throne and write your own faith declaration!

Nutrition Fit Tip:

Inflammation is the precursor to all chronic disease in the body. Changes in diet can greatly lower inflammation. Vegetables have a significant anti-inflammatory effect on the body as long as the person is not sensitive to them. Those with autoimmune conditions may need to eliminate some or all nightshade vegetables. Adding in healthy fats like olive, avocado and coconut oil also support healthy inflammatory responses, especially in the brain. Gluten and dairy are two of the most common foods that humans are sensitive to and can increase the inflammatory response.

CHANGE YOUR TUNE

Kathy Thorsen

"My anger will be kindled against them in that day. I will forsake them and hide my face from them; they will become easy prey, and many terrible troubles will come upon them. In that day they will say, 'Have not these troubles come upon us because our God is not in our midst?' Now therefore write this song, and teach it to the Israelites; put it in their mouths, in order that this song may be a witness for me against the Israelites. For when I have brought them into the land flowing with milk and honey, which I promised on oath to their ancestors, and they have eaten their fill and grown fat, they will turn to other gods and serve them, despising me and breaking my covenant."
~Deuteronomy 31:17, 19-20 (NRSVCE)

Have you ever had the lyrics to a song imprinted in your mind? The sense of hearing can become fixed in our memories and attached to events that hold importance in our lives. Our listening and lifestyle choices can either harmonize or create discord with our actions that ultimately become our destiny. Although we may not be able to get the song out of our head, we have the choice to either keep the music or pattern going or start moving to a different beat.

God created a song that incorporated specific instructions for the Israelites because He knew His words in this form would have a powerful influence and be passed down through the generations. He knew that the Israelites would not be able to resist their cravings. Once they had their fill of milk and honey, this prosperity minimized the past disciplinary actions of God and led them to make gods of their bellies and other false idols. Their addictions resonated so strongly throughout their physical bodies that His spirit and grace were no longer enough to change their tune. Initially, they tried to blame their misfortunes on God's absence, but—only upon taking responsibility of their own mistakes—did God provide the roadmap to recovery.

God already knows our woes and weaknesses and gives us plenty of healthy food, drink, instructional songs, and other resources to help us keep our covenant making God our number one idol. We just need to muster the courage to look honestly in the mirror, entertain His music, and make the change.

Thank You, God for continuing to teach me Your ways even though I often choose to satisfy the desires of my human body over the desire to please You. Forgive me for my attachment to addictive substances like sugar or alcohol and behaviors such as listening to gossip or profane lyrics that do not nourish my body or relationships. Help me to see what daily choices might be preventing me from following Your commands and make the necessary changes so that my family and future generations will see the power of Your mercy and loving guidance.   *Amen.*

Nutrition Of The Word

Have you ever succumbed to the cravings of the flesh even if you know they are not serving you or were breaking a covenant between you and a loved one? What food or habit is most likely to come between you and your love for God or others who need you? What song or Scripture might you sing out to God in petition for His aid to change you?

Nutrition Fit Tip:

If the flavor of olive oil is too strong for you, try avocado oil. It is rich in healthy fats and has a mild flavor. Use it to make you own mayonnaise or in a variety of salad dressings.

GOD IS WISE

Danelle Skinner

"Do not be wise in your own eyes; fear the LORD and shun evil. This will bring health to your body and nourishment to your bones."

~Proverbs 3:7-8 (NIV)

I used to be extremely self-centered and I had no idea I was even being that way. Despite having a very blessed life, I was almost listless; unhealthy, unnourished, and empty. I was trying to be self-sufficient, relying on my own inadequate wisdom to carry me through, but I was starving for true wisdom. It wasn't until I started to seek the Lord's wisdom by reading and studying the bible that my mental health returned, and my bones became nourished.

When we rely on our own wisdom, we are being self-centered... attempting to be self-sufficient and self-reliant. When we do this, we should fear the Lord because—in his eyes—self-dependency is prohibited. *"I can do all things through Christ who strengthens me."* (Philippians 4:13 NKJV) We cannot do all things without the wisdom of Christ! We must know God is the source of ALL wisdom. *"There is no wisdom and no understanding and no counsel against the Lord."* (Proverbs 21:30 NIV) If anything goes against God's wisdom it is false wisdom. *"It is the mark of the wise man that he fears the Lord and departs from evil."* (Proverbs 14:16 - NIV)

To trust in ourselves and our own wisdom is unwise. Godly wisdom comes directly from the Lord and it is revealed in His Word. When we read His Word, ask Him for wisdom, and depart from evil. God gives us His wisdom as a gift through the Holy Spirit. To receive this gift, we must first believe in Him, believe He cares for us, and believe He is able and willing to give us the wisdom we need!

God, Thank You for the nourishment of Your Living Word. Please help me to shun evil and self-reliance.

Amen.

NUTRITION OF THE WORD

God's wisdom brings health to your body and nourishment to your bones. Are you feeding yourself with the nutrient-dense Word of God or are you relying on yourself? Are your bones nourished by His wisdom? Jot down the areas of your life for which are you relying on your own wisdom instead of His and ask Him for wisdom in those areas, today.

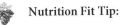 **Nutrition Fit Tip:**

Your mom was using wisdom when serving you chicken soup when you were sick! Learning to make bone broth is worth the time and effort. It is rich in minerals and collagen. Beef and especially veal bones make the richest and most nutritious stock. Bone broth freezes well and is convenient to have on hand for a quick soup or sauce base.

COME TO THE TABLE

Margaret Bentham-Moe

"All you people who are thirsty, come! Here is water for you to drink. Don't worry if you have no money. Come, eat and drink until you are full! You don't need money. The milk and wine are free."

~Isaiah 55:1 (ERV)

What if the highest-rated restaurant in the country announced that they would no longer be charging for dining there and everything would now be free. Could you imagine the response? We would use every form of communication to get the word out to our family and friends. Some may even camp out to be among the first in a line that would stretch as far as the eye could see. Undoubtedly, law enforcement would have to get involved to advert any ensuing unruliness, as persons from far and wide made their way there.

By contrast what's our response to exactly that invitation in Isaiah 55:1? Have we ourselves accepted it? And if we have, are we also excited enough to get the word out?

The sequence of Isaiah's invitation says a lot - it focuses first on thirst (which is symbolic dryness), before it tells us the cost (or lack thereof). In the natural, when we are really thirsty, we would desire water more than anything else. In the spiritual sense, before we can truly accept anything from the Lord, we must first accept that there is a thirst unlike any other; our very souls are parched and dry and the only hydration that will work is the Living Water Jesus gives. The Holy Spirit is the One who makes our reservation. The invitation does not set out any other criteria or qualification; we just have to want it. Secondly, the invitation declares that no money is needed and, indeed, no matter how much money we have, it cannot meet the longing of our souls. We cannot buy the things of God. We can't do anything to earn Grace, so we can all enjoy this freewill gift of a loving God and risen Savior and—with this knowledge—we can now feast on milk, which is indicative of the pure, wholesome, and sincere truth of God's Word, and the wine, representative of the covenant of our Heavenly Father and the joy that acceptance of this invitation brings.

Finally, once we've accepted the invitation, we need to invite others we come across in our daily lives. The people you see in your neighborhood and the places that you go every day. Teachers, neighbors, service people, homeless people, and others. It doesn't have to be formal "evangelism," but you should talk to others, invite them into conversation, and tell them about God. The people on the highways and by-ways of your walk with God. Be the body of Christ there. Everybody has a place in God's Creation. Invite them to the table with you!

Father thank You so much for Your invitation freely extended to all to quench the longing of our souls to feast at Your table and know the joy of Your salvation. Help us, Holy Spirit, to always say yes. In Jesus Name.

Amen.

Are you ready to accept this wonderful invitation? If you are not ready, what situation in your life do you feel would hinder you from saying yes? Who do you need to reach out to, in order to invite that person to join you at God's table?

_____
_____
_____
_____
_____
_____
_____
_____
_____
_____
_____
_____
_____
_____
_____
_____
_____
_____
_____
_____

Nutrition Fit Tip:

Roasted vegetables are a delicious way to enjoy more vegetables in your diet. Toss a variety with olive oil and roast in a 400-degree oven until tender. Onions, peppers, garlic cloves zucchini and eggplant work well, but any will do. Eat them right out of the oven or puree them and add to chili or marinara sauce or use as a base for a vegetable soup.

Surrender Your "Stash"

Lisa Danegelis

"The grass withers, the flower fades, but the word of our God stands forever."
~Isaiah 40: 8 (NKJV)

"Sugar is slowly killing you." Talk about something a professional baker doesn't want to hear!

I spread the love with food. I also am a sugar addict. It was becoming clear how toxic sugar was to my system. My shrinking jeans, brain fog, and body aches spoke volumes. Efforts to stop had been mediocre at best; I needed to fully surrender. (Or so I thought.) So, sugar and I broke up. Well, let's say we tried. Being a recovering overachiever, I dove in, gave my "stash" away and hunkered down for the fight. Soon after, I realized I was thinking about sugar more than when I was when consuming it!

I felt imprisoned!

Wisdom was downloaded as an answer to my fervent prayers. Over the next several days God made it clear to me that sugar was not my enemy, my misplaced loyalty was. Sugar had been the quick fix for negative emotions and the false bandage for the heartaches that needed God's salve. This idol had taken a piece of my heart that should have been reserved for God.

I now know it wasn't sugar that was "killing me," it was my overindulgence and idolatry of it. It was bringing a slow death to a part of my soul. Sugar and I still meet up occasionally, but the only "god" I will run to in desperate times will be the One True God who holds the throne.

His words, whether they be whispered to our soul or read, are His best for us. In the craziness of this world, let His simple nudges be your compass. As with His whisper to me, His words may seem cryptic at first - easily misunderstood. God's mysterious ways draw us into intimacy with Him as we search for deeper truths. His Word and our obedience will be all that matters when this world is forgotten. His Word stands forever.

Father forgive me for putting anything other than You on the throne of my life. Help me to solidify Your Word in my heart and run only to You when I hurt.

Amen.

Is there something you have not surrendered to God? Maybe it is a bad habit, a material possession or even a relationship. Has God given you a few reminders and you are still resisting? Write about what you may lose if you chose to obey and also what you know you will gain.

_____
_____
_____
_____
_____
_____
_____
_____
_____
_____
_____
_____
_____
_____
_____
_____
_____
_____
_____
_____
_____
_____

 Nutrition Fit Tip:

Avoiding preservatives is an important part of clean eating. Instead of purchasing the coconut milk in the refrigerated section which has added ingredients, purchase full fat canned coconut milk. Put it in a shaker bottle and dilute with 2-3 parts water. Use this in your specialty coffee drinks.

ALL OF HIS WORDS ARE TRUTH

Marlene Dawson

"There is therefore now no condemnation for those who are in Christ Jesus. For the law of the Spirit of life in Christ Jesus has set you free from the law of sin and death."

~ Romans 8:1-2 (NASB)

My testimony is one of coming out of guilt and condemnation for lies and abuses I believed were my fault. Even though I became a Christian at nineteen, it would be years before I received the truth of freedom from sin committed against me. I was nearly thirty when I discovered I asked Jesus into my heart at Vacation Bible School when I was four years old. I was sure my sin was too great to be covered by His cross. Bible verses that spoke of freedom did not ring true for me, as I was still bound in condemnation. Even though I read the Bible and believed the salvation words, I was disconnected from words of freedom. I could not talk about being abused because I believed it was all my fault; something had to be terribly wrong with me for my daddy to do that. No matter how often I tried to chew on the freedom words, I spit them out because it seemed to have no relevance for me.

Then I heard Billy Graham say, "the whole Bible is the truth, so you can believe it," and I was determined to believe what God said.

In choosing to believe God's word, Romans 8:1-2 are meaty verses. We have to break them into smaller pieces to assimilate them. We must believe that we are no longer condemned because we are now in Christ. It may take years to digest the truth of verse one.

As we chew on verse two, we may vacillate between what God has said, and what we have done. *'Free from the law of sin and death? Lord, do you know what happened? How can this be reconciled?'*

His answer is always the same, "In Jesus."

Christ's finished work on the cross is the bridge between our sinful places and His holy place. We learn to partake of His divine nature, first at His cross, then at His throne.

Dear Lord, I know Your word is truth. Please help me believe and receive all Your finished work. Thank You, Lord.

Amen.

Nutrition Of The Word

We come to Jesus Christ in our places of brokenness. What lie have you believed that has kept you from honest communication and relationships? Where have you kept God at arm's length? How will you invite Him to take His place on the throne of your heart?

_____

_____

_____

_____

_____

_____

_____

_____

_____

_____

_____

_____

_____

_____

_____

_____

_____

_____

_____

_____

Nutrition Fit Tip:

When counting carbs, make sure you consider adding in small amounts of legumes such as lentils, black beans, and chickpeas. They are packed with protein, fiber and prebiotics (prebiotics feed the already present helpful bacteria in your gut).

Hidden Clues

Tamara Fink

> "He humbled you and let you be hungry, and fed you with manna which you did not know, nor did your fathers know, that He might make you understand that man does not live by bread alone, but man lives by everything that proceeds out of the mouth of the LORD."
>
> ~Deuteronomy 8:3 (NIV)

There have been times in my life when I haven't understood why God allowed such agonizing pain. One of those times was during college. I was in a relationship that I had really hoped would be my happily ever after love story. I trusted God with the relationship, yet still experienced incredible heartache when it didn't work out. I was sad for a long time. I cried out, *'Why God? Why didn't you intervene and stop this pain?'*

Reading this passage of scripture, I can only imagine the pain the Israelites were feeling. Even more shocking was when I realized God didn't just allow the Israelites to be humbled, He initiated the humbling. These were His chosen people. They had been slaves that He miraculously freed and now they were wandering aimlessly in the wilderness…or so it seemed. Reading further about the Israelites you'll see they weren't wandering at all. They were being led by a cloud during the day and fire at night. God hadn't left them. He was intentionally doing this and He wasn't done. He allowed them to go hungry as well. It's evident He was teaching them something, but what?

One thing I love about God's word is that it's full of clues. The definition of manna is one of those clues: it's an unknown provision that one must look up for. God gave the Israelites an incredible gift during the wait. They learned to be fully dependent on Him for their everything. He is the God who provides, Jehovah-Jireh. He gave them an unknown provision, a provision that they knew nothing of, but it met their needs.

Little did I know during my time of hurting that God had my forever mate already in mind for me. He had a provision for me about which I knew nothing, but I would have to trust Him to provide.

Lord Jesus, thank You for your provision. Thank You for being faithful to meet all of my needs. Today I will listen for Your voice and trust Your leading, because You are my faithful God.

Amen.

Nutrition Of The Word

How often do we want to know God's plan? How often do we struggle in the waiting? What have you learned from a wilderness wandering experience yourself?

_____
_____
_____
_____
_____
_____
_____
_____
_____
_____
_____
_____
_____
_____
_____
_____
_____
_____
_____
_____
_____

 Nutrition Fit Tip:

Adding flaxseed meal to your soups, stews and baked goods is an excellent way to consume more healthy fats and add much needed fiber.

BLOSSOM WITH THE FOOD OF GOD

Margaret Bentham-Moe

"Give us the food we need for today."

~Matthew 6:11 (ERV)

I love plants and can actually be seen speaking to them. There's this particular plant that started out quite lovely when I bought it, but—over time—became little more than a skinny stick with straggling leaves. I really didn't see much sense in giving it more than a daily dash of water convinced that it had seen its best days. Recently, I decided to put plant food into the soil of the skinny stick on a regular basis but still wasn't really expecting anything much and especially not the nice green leaves and purple flowers that have appeared. When I got it right, the plant benefited tremendously; food for thought wouldn't you say?

Thank God He provides us with the right daily provision, all we have to do is ask. Wherever we are in our walk with the Lord, babes or mature Christians, God—through His Living Word—provides both milk and meat. This verse from the Lord's Prayer also connotes whatever is needed for today, it's all encompassing. Both rich and poor must ask God for daily food; because the well-off may not require literal food, we see clearly that God's provision is not limited to what we eat. Daily meditating on the Word of God is the food that our spirit needs. When I treat my Bible reading as I did the watering of that skinny stick of a plant, I may sprout a few scriptures here and there but I fail to live in the fullness of what Jesus gave His life for me to enjoy.

In asking food of our Father He does not only give us what delights the eyes and fills the belly, but also what enriches our souls and gives us the ability to fight battles that may be thrown our way. The Hebrew word for food has a very interesting meaning. Originating from the root word "Zayin," which means a weapon or a sword, it's connected to the Hebrew word "mazon," which is food, sustenance, nourishment.

Food is our weapon for daily life.

Unlike my now blossoming plant that had to wait on me to provide what's necessary for it to thrive, God says to us, just ask. What are we waiting for?

Father You have provided everything for life and Godliness. Help us to seek You daily and to know that You have already provided for our every need. In Jesus Name.

Amen.

Is there any situation in your life that is like my stick plant, dying and seemingly beyond recovery? Ask God's help in nourishing the situation and write down the promise, verse, or words He gives you, while in this prayer. Feed frequently on His promise by reading it often, posting it around your home, and saying it aloud.

 Nutrition Fit Tip:

Eat foods that are closest to their natural state as possible. When all else fails, just aim to eat whole, fresh foods in a rainbow of colors. Avoid any food that has more than three or four ingredients on the label. Want to live longer? Eat foods without labels!

MORE THAN ENOUGH

Teresa Kliner

"The steadfast love of the Lord never ceases; his mercies never come to an end; they are new every morning; great is your faithfulness."

~Lamentations 3:22,23 (NIV)

The other day, I was so excited about going to a leadership conference. I had finally started to believe that God had something for me. I was expecting Him to show up and give me something special. When my best friend texted me to say that she was going to this conference as well, at first, I was excited to spend time together and share this experience with her. And about two seconds later, I had the thought, *'Crap....now God is going to give her something special instead of me!'*

How lame is that! Like really?

> I believe God is the God of the Universe.
> I believe He made the world in six days.
> I believe He died and rose again.
> I believe He walked on water.
> I believe He heals the blind.

But I didn't believe He would have enough for both me and my friend? I somehow thought that—when it came time to pouring out His spirit and His blessings—He would somehow run out just before He got to me?

He has more than enough power to sustain each and every one of us. He is faithful and His mercies are new every morning. His love never ends which means that He has more than enough for me, my friend and everyone else in the universe all at the same time.

Lord, forgive me for putting You in a box. Forgive me for not believing that You are who You say You are. Thank you that even when we are faithless You are faithful. Help me to remember today that Your love for me is never ending.

Amen.

If I'm honest, this definitely wasn't this first time I put a cap on God. How often do you limit God? How often do you assume there isn't enough for you? What can you start to believe God bigger for in your life?

Nutrition Fit Tip:

For a simple creamy dairy free soup, sauté onions and chopped peeled butternut squash in olive oil. Cook until tender and add full fat coconut milk, curry powder and season with salt and pepper. Puree in a blender. Add sautéed shrimp or roasted chicken for a full meal. There is no need to use thickening agents such as unhealthy flour and cornstarch when preparing soup this way. The pureed vegetables themselves act as the thickener. Experiment with asparagus, tomatoes, cauliflower and different seasonings.

A Full Portion Of Perfect Provision

Jane Guffy

> "And bring the fattened calf and kill it, and let us eat and celebrate."
>
> ~Luke 15:23 (ESV)

Let's set the table!

Meal planning is so easy. I don't even have to "plan;" the backup options are plentiful. I consider shopping or eating out. I decide what sounds good, make a list, head to the grocery store of choice, fill a cart, and check out. They even bag it. My cabinets, refrigerator, and freezer are stocked. I rinse, chop, cook, and serve. I know who is coming for dinner, how many there will be, and I set the time. No barn. No pasture out back. No live animals to slaughter to accommodate a surprise arrival. Pretty planned and controlled.

This special day was the homecoming of a lost, pride-filled son to his father. The father who had willingly given something up. This faithful, loving father had been fasting from the presence of his son. The celebration of the son who chose to wander, was lost, and is now found. The father's call to bring the fattened calf was a call to celebrate and feast with abundance. God's provision for man to have the resources of this earth to feed, nourish, and sustain our physical bodies is noteworthy. It's His perfect plan of provision.

God's plan to provide and care for us is complete. Bring "the" fattened calf also indicates that there was just one: a single, special, fattened calf to feed with jubilee. It must have been a clearly recognizable calf! The fattened calf represents Christ who is our spiritual nourishment. God has given us Jesus to endlessly feast and be filled with. A full portion! No drive-through service. Planned and delivered to us!

God I am so filled with gratitude for the gift of food for my body that You made. Thank You for the sacrifice of Jesus, the fattened calf, so my life would be full and worthy of celebration.

Amen.

Nutrition Of The Word

What homecomings do you celebrate with great joy? What has the Lord brought back to you, fattened with fullness that fills you up?

_____
_____
_____
_____
_____
_____
_____
_____
_____
_____
_____
_____
_____
_____
_____
_____
_____
_____
_____
_____

Nutrition Fit Tip:

Prepare a large batch of homemade mayonnaise using olive oil or avocado oil. Use it as a base for preservative free ranch dressing, Caesar dressing, tartar sauce, Thousand Island dressing, and more! It keeps for several weeks in your refrigerator and the uses are endless!

Don't Look Down

Kathy Carter

"I have told you these things so that in me you may have peace. You will have suffering in this world. Be courageous. I have conquered the world."

~John 16:33 (CSB)

Fear once literally stopped me in the middle of the French Alps, on a college ski trip! Never having been in France, skied a mountains slope, or rode on a Button Lift, this particular fear was all new to me and very real. Your feet are kept in a track on a button lift and you are pushed up the steep mountains. My ski got out of the track and I was pulled off the lift at a little more than halfway up the mountain. My buddies all continued the journey up and I ended up in a steep, rocky, and non-skiable area. I felt paralyzed, hopeless, lost and alone. I only had myself to rely on and my spirit was crumbled. I just kept saying to myself, "don't look down." I slid on my bottom for safety, making my way toward an actual run and blocking the path for experienced skiers making their way down this difficult slope as they cursed at me in a language I did not understand.

Fortunately, I am here today to share my story and reflect on my feelings. I went from feeding my mind with hopeless thoughts about giving up to courageous, positive words about finding a way. I wish back then I would've known Jesus like I do today. Little did I know, God was there with me, sending peace and strength my way.

In John 16:33, God is telling us to look to Him for peace, strength, support, and comfort. We will have interruptions in life that will bring fear and tribulation. Be strong and courageous. Christ has overcome the world and He will put His overcoming spirit into our weakness; His super on our natural! Be reliant on God and fix your eyes on Him. Don't look down. Look to faith to overcome fear.

Thank You, God, for feeding our mind with courage through Your strength and support. Thank You for always being with us in our trials and adversities. I promise to turn to You Lord in times of fear and rely on Your strength to get me through. In Your name, Lord Jesus Christ.

Amen.

Visualize yourself in the most fearful circumstance in your life. What does that look like? Now visualize yourself conquering that fear. What steps did you take and what was the result? If God were in the picture, how would it feel?

 Nutrition Fit Tip:

Make a delicious dairy-free sauce by pureeing avocados, fresh basil, pine nuts, lemon and garlic. Slowly drizzle in olive oil to make a creamy nutrient dense sauce to toss with zucchini noodles or serve over grilled fish.

EXERCISE YOUR FAITH

*Just as there are many forms of physical exercise, there are many ways that a woman will **Exercise Her Faith** as she walks with God.*

The Word of God does not call us to inactivity. Rather, it calls us to playing an active role in bringing God's Kingdom to the earth and it takes our faith "muscle" to do it.

During our journey to becoming Holy, Whole, and Fit, we will be led by the Spirit to Exercise Our Faith in many different ways; thanksgiving, using our gifts, acts of service to others, trusting, believing, praying, speaking the truth in love, and forgiving, to name a few. Even rest can be an Exercise of Faith when what we would prefer to do is make something happen for ourselves!

Serving God will never be boring and it will require exercise for our spiritual health. Just like exercise increases the body's endurance and effectiveness, so exercising our faith makes us "strong in the Lord and in the power of His might."

It is our prayer that these writings would cause you to increase the amount of exercise your faith "muscle" is getting and you will see God's Kingdom at work in your own life and with your own eyes.

FUEL YOUR SOUL

Tamara Fink

> "I press on toward the goal for the prize of the upward call of God in Christ Jesus."
>
> ~Philippians 3:14 (NIV)

New Year's Eve comes every year but I was determined this year would mark the year my pre-baby body would make its comeback. I got a gym membership and was determined to learn clean eating. I was prepared and knew that my fat would melt away and my atrophied muscles would tone right up. You probably already know where this is going…. By the fourth week, I had lost my excitement and life had gotten in the way of my plan. One day, while working out, I became extremely lightheaded and had to stop. I realized—in my attempts to regain the desired body—I had deprived myself of the fuel I needed to perform the workout I was doing.

As I worked my hidden ab muscles on an exercise ball I heard this voice in my spirit whisper, *'this is just like running your race with me. If you haven't feasted on my Word you cannot run the race to receive my prize.'*

Wow! Does that speak to you like it spoke to me? I was ready to begin exercising my faith and I God told me that it worked hand-in-hand with the *Nutrition of the Word.*

I had been "pressing on" with my exercising, but I hadn't been fueling my body to ensure its effectiveness to complete the goal and win the prize.

"Complete the goal" and "win the prize" are two different things. The goal is the destination, while the prize is what is attained upon completion. God has already done the work to ensure we reach our goal by sending His Son to die on the cross for our salvation. However, there is a prize to be attained as well. This prize cannot be attained without self-care. Once we have ingested His Word, it's time to *Exercise our Faith*!

Our bodies are His temple and how He is able to do His work though us. We are not vain to want to take care of our bodies. Without self-care, which is nourished—above all—through His Word, we'll never accomplish the plans God has for us. We must run our race, *Exercise our Faith*, with our spirits fully nourished by His Word, our ears attuned to His voice and our eyes on the goal.

Lord Jesus, thank You for attaining the ultimate goal for me. Please remind me to stay fully nourished on Your Word daily, as I press on to win the prize and live out the call You have placed on my life.

Amen.

Exercise Your Faith

Have you experienced a time when you pressed on for a goal only to realize you hadn't fed your soul first? With a well-nourished soul, what is God calling you to, in order to *Exercise Your Faith*?

_____
_____
_____
_____
_____
_____
_____
_____
_____
_____
_____
_____
_____
_____
_____
_____
_____
_____
_____
_____

Exercise Fit Tip:

You can protect your body and speed up post workout recovery time by eating foods that help prevent inflammation. Some great ideas include moringa oleifera, broccoli, tuna, and avocado.

OUR BORROWED STRUCTURES

Kathy Thorsen

> "Do you not know that your body is a temple of the Holy Spirit within you, which you have from God? You are not your own; you were bought with a price. So glorify God in your body."
>
> ~1 Corinthians 6:19-20 (RSVCE)

After my diagnosis of a chronic autoimmune disease, the realization that my body was vulnerable and previous life choices contributed to the weakened bodily state hit me like a brick. How many times had I not respected the one sacred temple afforded by God within which my soul resides? I was led to believe, by society, that my physical health would not be affected by an occasional binge. It was also easy to believe, from advertisements, that what I put on my skin or exposed my body to when cleaning or working around the home would never tarnish the inner functions of my precious human body. How about all the days where I chose to sit in front of the television or computer all day without taking breaks to walk or stretch, parked as close to the store as possible, or skipped my exercise class because I felt like I did not have time or the energy to honor the innate need to move. It is easy to take for granted this amazing gift God has purchased for each one of us with the blood of His own son.

Though we would like to believe we are immortal, our bodies are just a borrowed structure within which our spirit lives. We often create unhealthy habits because we believe exercising discipline in our daily choices is not necessary to optimize how our bodies function. Like professional athletes who execute self-discipline daily to be worthy of their places on the team, every little step we take to create a well maintained dwelling place for the Holy Spirit will demonstrate respect for the God who has paid the ultimate price for our existence.

We owe it to God to take responsibility for everything we put in and on His temple, as well as exercise daily discipline to maintain optimum function so that the bodies He purchased for us are capable of carrying out His plan.

Thank You, God, for this magnificent body which I may have taken for granted in the past. Grant me the courage to honestly evaluate and execute where I need to make changes in my daily habits to maximize my ability to fulfill my purpose in this life.

Amen.

When was the last time you made taking care of your body a priority over taking care of some material possession? What area of your life needs the most attention to create a temple fit for God? What are you willing to change in your daily lifestyle habits to demonstrate respect and gratitude to God?

___

Exercise Fit Tip:

Exercise twenty minutes daily five days each week will extend life expectancy ten years. You do not have to kill yourself running, jogging, etc. Walking provides incredible health benefits!

God's Healing Words

Susan Brozek

"….But just say the word, and my servant will be healed."
~Matthew 8:8 (NIV)

How many of us, in the midst of our busy lives, really take the time to quiet ourselves before the Lord, and give Him ample opportunity to speak into our hearts? This is not only a challenge, but a spiritual discipline. Amidst all of the distractions that we face, it is often difficult to be still and simply listen to Him speak to us. Technology. Family demands. Job requirements. Household maintenance and upkeep. I believe that very few of us have trouble giving God a list of our needs, wants, and petitions...which is, of course, entirely acceptable. But our God is a God of relationship, and a relationship involves two-way communication. He wants us to give Him the chance to guide us with His "still, small voice." His words come down and take root in our hearts, which then become a catalyst for healing within us.

The power of God speaking breaks bondages and strongholds. God speaks to us every time we open His Word, but He also speaks to us about the attributes of who He is, and the characteristics of our identity in Him. He speaks directly and personally about our life path and decisions we need to make. Being guided by Christ is one of the most powerful and transformational elements of our walk that we can receive from God as He speaks to us in His Word.

Will you listen when He speaks, as He did in these examples?

I am able to do all things through Christ. – Philippians 4:13
I am guided. – Psalms 48:14
I am given all things. – Romans 8:32
I am more than a conqueror. – Romans 8:37
My eyes are fixed on Jesus – Hebrews 12:2
I am walking worthy of God's calling. – Ephesians 4:1
I am reigning in life. – Romans 5:17
I am led in Christ's triumph. – 2 Corinthians 2:14

Father God, help me to not only quiet myself frequently that I may hear Your still small voice speaking to me, but also enable me to embrace who You say I am.

Amen.

Exercise Your Faith

Today's journaling assignment is simple. Don't let Satan engage in "identity theft" in your life for one more day. *Exercise Your Faith* by writing out the corresponding Scripture verses listed above. Then ponder these truths about who you are in Christ.

_____
_____
_____
_____
_____
_____
_____
_____
_____
_____
_____
_____
_____
_____
_____
_____
_____
_____
_____
_____

 **Exercise Fit Tip:**

Exercise encourages the formation of new neurons in the brain. Regular exercise increases volumes of gray and white matter in the brain and can help prevent cognitive decline.

STOP HINDERING YOUR RUN

Tamara Fink

> "Therefore, since we have so great a cloud of witnesses surrounding us, let us also lay aside every encumbrance and the sin which so easily entangles us, and let us run with endurance the race that is set before us."
>
> ~Hebrews 12:1 (NIV)

I wouldn't consider myself a runner. I have done a couple of 5Ks, half marathons, and a Tough Mudder, but not because I like running. I actually despise it. However, there is nothing like the adrenaline rush of being out of there with all of the other athletes waiting for the gun to go off. Everyone starts out together and, eventually, you all find your pace and settle in. As the miles tick by, you begin to notice sweatshirts and pants strewn along the streets from athletes shedding the extra layers that are no longer needed. My favorite part of the race, even better than the finish line, is the encouragement. Veteran runners are frequently caught encouraging new runners to keep going and there are complete strangers lining the streets cheering and waving banners. In that moment, I don't despise running anymore. I'm energized and proud to be one of the contenders.

Having had those race experiences, the author's words make sense to me. Our race of life has been set and the heavenly witnesses are ready to cheer us on, but they can't run our race for us. The actual running is up to us. As I pondered what it was that made me despise running so much, I realized I was afraid of failing, looking foolish, and making myself uncomfortable. How similar is that with our faith journey? Fear of failure is a ploy of the enemy to make us forget that God has already secured our destination. We can't fail when we accept him as our Savior. Looking foolish is only a concern when we're striving for the accolades of man. There is so much freedom in knowing He created me, loves me and has a plan for my life. His accolades are all I desire. And my flesh being uncomfortably starved …well let's be honest, that is good if my spirit man is flourishing. To lay aside those hindrances and run my race for Christ is total freedom!

Lord, please show me what I need to throw off so I can run my race unencumbered for You. I'm so grateful that You have set my course. Teach me to trust You, Jesus.

Amen.

What is holding you back or slowing you down from running your race? Who can you come alongside and encourage to continue running their race and not quit?

 Exercise Fit Tip:

Lay out your workout clothes, as well as your professional outfit before you go to bed so you have no excuse not to work out in the morning because you ran out of time.

YOU ARE GIFTED—SUPERNATURALLY!

Kimberly Joy Krueger

> "There are different kinds of gifts. But they are all given to believers by the same Spirit. There are different ways to serve. But they all come from the same Lord."
>
> ~1 Corinthians 12:4-5 (NIRV)

I am blessed to work with women every day and I am astounded by how many of them don't believe that they are gifted in any way. Women with this mindset far outnumber those who understand that they possess gifts given by God and were created for greatness. The enemy has sold us a lie: we are not gifted; we are nothing special. I can tell you exactly how that lie is so easily bought. Satan simply turns our focus onto ourselves; onto our limited natural abilities and our many weaknesses. Once we believe we're not gifted, then it follows that we're not special, because that's what the world believes. It takes no time at all for us to believe we have very little to offer the world, much less God.

But the gifts we are given by the Lord are not given to make us special. We are already special! Our specialness was proven on the Cross of Christ! We are the object of the most sacrificial and extravagant love ever shown—you can't get any more special than that! No, the gifts given to each believer are not for specialness, but for service. We are called to serve with our gifts and our call is not from this world. Neither are the gifts we will need to fulfill that call!

That is why Paul is not talking about our natural abilities here! He is telling us that the Holy Spirit has put His "super" on our "natural" and His "extra" on our "ordinary"—and that He does this for every believer. Are you a believer? Then you are, in fact, gifted—supernaturally! You are extraordinary, equipped and able! The question is: Will you believe the truth of God's Word over the lies Satan and the world have told you? Will you believe the Holy Spirit has placed His gifts in you and answer His call to serve today?

Lord, I believe You've placed Your gifts in me. Help my unbelief! Show me what my gifts are, so that I may use them to serve others and bring much glory to Your Wonderful Name!

Amen.

Exercise Your Faith

What God says about you is the truest thing about you. What truth from these scriptures overrule what you've believed about yourself? What gifts do you think the Holy Spirit has placed in you? What does it look like for you to "answer the call" on your life?

_____
_____
_____
_____
_____
_____
_____
_____
_____
_____
_____
_____
_____
_____
_____
_____
_____
_____
_____
_____

Exercise Fit Tip:

Holy yoga embraces the essential elements of yoga: breath work, meditation and physical postures with Christ as the focus of intention and worship. Look for a holy yoga class near you.

"COME!"

Jane Guffy

"He said, 'Come.' So Peter got out of the boat and walked on the water and came to Jesus."

~Matthew 14:29 (ESV)

I have a dog. I cannot count how many times I say "come." It's said forcefully with expectation that he respond and do what I say the first time. When my five kids were young, I called them, "come here." The dog, the kids, and (if I'm honest) I don't always want to come when called. Choosing to come when called means making a decision, taking action, and moving. My call to come is usually forceful, sometimes with annoyance, and probably demanding.

Jesus says, "Come," to Peter. One simple four-letter word with huge impact, consequence, and deliverance. In this story, Peter was being called to come out of the boat onto, not into, the water. I image a gentle, confidence inspiring, trustworthy voice when Jesus said "come." That's a bold call to come . . . out onto the waters in vulnerability. Faith and fear cannot coexist. Decision time! Peter chose to *Exercise His Faith*! Peter's step-count on his spiritual Fitbit went way up that evening.

When we are called by God to come follow Him, do we hesitate, or step right out of our dry, comfortable, predictable place, into and onto the unknown waters? Peter stepped out! He answered the call, regardless of the conditions. He was clearly stepping out in trust of Jesus.

Each act of obedience is like a callisthenic strengthening our desire to put our faith into action. Sometimes the call to come is loud and clear. Other times it's a whisper. Are we listening?

We are each called to come do our part for high impact in God's Kingdom. He knows where we are weak and need to be reinforced. He's our personal trainer for our faith muscle. He has a plan for how to best exercise us, in order to build our strength and endurance.

Lord God, thank You for the call the "come." Please never allow my faith muscle to atrophy. Use me. Build into me. Train me to hear, come, and follow.

Amen.

Exercise Your Faith

What are you doing to protect your faith muscle from atrophy? When have you answered the call to come and how did it help your heart health?

 **Exercise Fit Tip:**

Never go more than two days in a row without exercise. Even on vacation, look for many fun options! Be creative!

Exercise Your Faith With Joy!

Rebecca Grambort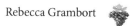

> "Consider it pure joy, my brothers and sisters, whenever you face trials of many kinds, because you know that the testing of your faith produces perseverance. Let perseverance finish its work so that you may be mature and complete, not lacking anything."
>
> ~James 1:2-4 (NIV)

"Consider it pure joy?" Have you ever questioned God about the human ability to choose joy in the face of seemingly unbearable trials?

I remember a time when I questioned my ability to, not only choose joy, but my capacity to persevere. I was okay with God perfecting His work in me, but there were things that I would prefer to avoid in the process. Back when my husband was gravely ill, I was paging through scripture for comfort, when this verse challenged me. I cried out to God, *'Is this a test? I know you want to grow me up, but please not this way. I commit to praising you in this storm, just please spare my husband.'*

I bargained as I prayed. Can you relate?

Through the written Word, God is encouraging us to stay the course through these hardships that test our faith. We must surrender ourselves to Him so that He can finish the work that He started in us. There isn't an easy way out and living from a position of praise without question is the key ingredient to pressing through our trials. In this process, He grows us up so that we do not stay childlike forever. We are to be sons and daughters and so He must carve into us Christ-like characteristics such as perseverance, so that we may become mature and complete, lacking nothing. What is the lack that He speaks of? Well – most of all – Him!

If God would spare us from these trials, we would never have the privilege to become intimately acquainted with Jesus and become more like Him. Trials strip away the world. We have to depend on Him. He becomes our securities. Nothing down here is safe. He is where we are going. This is why He says to; *"Consider it pure joy."*

Knowing Him is pure joy!

Jesus, I will consider it pure joy! I do not want to stay child-like forever. I will surrender myself to You, so that You can make me mature and complete, lacking nothing.

Amen.

Exercise Your Faith

Many people wish that good health and fitness came without having to do the hard work. However, that's just not reality. Like exercise for our bodies, we also need to *Exercise Our Faith*. When we are stretched, we are strengthened and that takes perseverance! In what ways can you choose joy so that persevering becomes easier for you in your process of becoming mature and complete, not lacking anything?

Exercise Fit Tip:

Make your own workout playlist! Your favorite music will distract you from boredom, motivate you, and keep you on track.

Step Toward The Light

Kathy Carter

"Don't you know that the runners in a stadium all race, but only one receives the prize? Run in such a way to win the prize."

~1 Corinthians 9:24 (CSB)

Competing in the Hawaiian Ironman Triathlon was never on my radar. Top proven athletes are chosen to compete in this race. Why was I chosen? Did God have a plan to use this race to strengthen my race with Him? Did He know I would look back at the Ironman race—the 2.4 mile fight against waves and salty waters, the near defeatist feeling pedaling against extreme side winds on the 112 mile bike, and finally persevering through the 26.2 mile marathon in the dark—and relate it to God's race? My goal in the triathlon was to just keep moving forward to the next set of bright lights in the distance; the bright, warm smiles and welcoming hands at each mile aid station.

Similar to finishing an Ironman, there are many hurdles to staying the course with God: Commitment to God's Word every day, putting His words into action, following the voice of the Holy Spirit and not the enemy, and serving others.

During my Ironman race, I remember a voice whispering, *'Don't give up, keep stepping, stay strong, the light is up ahead.'* Was it my voice or His?

In 1 Corinthians 9:24, there were no medals for those who merely finished the race, only for the first to cross the finish line. In our faith, the aim is not victory so much as a particular way of running the race. We should run the race with the kind of effort and dedication victory requires.

Let us all run our race with the effort of winning! Even when we have doubts that we will finish, God is always holding our hand and guiding us toward the medal of victory. Stay the course and keep stepping toward God's light. With the help of His trusting hand, you will reach the golden pathway to Heaven and the Promised Land. You will receive that finisher's medal.

Dear God, Thank You for the lesson to run Your race with persistency so that we can reach the gift of eternity with You.

Amen.

Exercise Your Faith

Envision a time when you felt like quitting because the end was nowhere in sight? What process did you use to conquer your doubt and accomplish the task? If you are still feeling uncertain, how will you trust God to help you finish strong?

_____
_____
_____
_____
_____
_____
_____
_____
_____
_____
_____
_____
_____
_____
_____
_____
_____
_____
_____
_____
_____
_____
_____

 Exercise Fit Tip:

You are more likely to achieve your fitness goals when you have an accountability partner for support.

Rise And Go To The Father

Jane Guffy

"I will rise and go to my father, and I will say to him, 'Father, I have sinned against heaven and before you.'"

~Luke 15:18 (ESV)

Few things can be more difficult and humbling than admitting I'm wrong. I consider whether to email a letter of explanation or face it in person. Next, I consider timing. Timing: it's usually to benefit me and how my confession will be received. Lots of stuff about me in that. I protect myself. I'll go so far as to attempt to justify my actions, in order to dilute my need to fully confess.

The priority of protection over being truly humble and repenting isn't exercising my faith. It is selfish, lacking in trust, and doesn't lean on faith at all. It places faith in a second-string line-up. Benched.

God uses the prodigal son to teach about the power of asking for forgiveness by training through the flexing of the most important muscle - the heart. Step 1 - He rises to the occasion. I can almost picture him going from a slouched position to standing with a new purpose. I'll bet his heart rate went into fat burn mode! Next, the statement "I will," is determination. "Go."

There you have it! No hesitation. No timing consideration. He gave thought to what he needed to do to achieve his goal. He confessed sin to our heavenly Father, the one he wronged. The prodigal son had his eyes on the prize. He planned his work and worked his plan. The confession of his sin had to have felt like the barbells hitting the floor after holding those weights over his head. His plan built his faith muscle to bear the weight of sin and lift it up to his Father. Rise. Go. Say.

Heavenly Father, Your grace is immeasurable. The opportunities for me to put my faith into action are endless. I ask that You lead me in exercising my faith in Your never-ending mercy, sprint into action, lunge to the foot of the cross, and run Your race well.

Amen.

Exercise Your Faith

Consider and list the ways your faith is strengthened by unloading the weight of your sin through power lifting your confession to God.

___

 Exercise Fit Tip:

Set a goal to motivate you to workout. For instance, registering for a 5K walk or run will motivate you to train.

Discipline And Winning Go Hand-in-Hand

Margaret Bentham-Moe

"For that reason, I don't run just for exercise or box like one throwing aimless punches, but I train like a champion athlete. I subdue my body and get it under my control, so that after preaching the good news to others I myself won't be disqualified."

~1 Corinthians 9:26-27 (TPT)

The Olympic Games are arguably the greatest display of athletes who've trained for their big moment. I've never seen anyone slated for a particular event attempting to run a different race or casually sauntering down the track at the sound of the starting gun. Each is focused on winning the event at hand. This passage of scripture teaches that discipline and winning go hand-in-hand and—while important for athletes—it's critical for our walk with the Lord.

I've read and heard this scripture many times, but I must confess that the reality of what's at stake never hit home. Many questions come to mind such as; *'Am I running the disciplined Christian life that Paul wrote about?' 'Have I subdued my body and brought it under my control (note the personal responsibility)?'*

Sometimes I've tried to run different races at the same time, "multi-tasking," I claim. Inconsequential, perhaps, when it comes to the do-it-yourself items left unfinished, or the book that may not be read in its entirety; yet, we must endeavor to finish what we've started as my Apostle always says to "be a finisher." There's no area as important for us to be finishers as in the race for eternal life. From our starting point at the Cross of our Lord and Savior Jesus Christ, to the finish line at the Throne of our Heavenly Father, we cannot allow ourselves to be side-tracked. The solution is actually our total dependence on the Person of the Holy Spirit.

Just as athletes need a coach to help them achieve their goals, we also need one to help us keep our eyes on the prize. Jesus said it was better for us that He should go so that the Holy Spirit could come. We cannot afford to find ourselves castaways; that will only be avoided if we listen to the wisdom of our personal trainer, the Holy Spirit.

Father, You have given us everything we need to finish our race. By Your Grace may we help those we meet along the way to know our Lord Jesus and the sweet fellowship of the Holy Spirit. In Jesus name.

Amen.

Exercise Your Faith

Which question about God's stakes resonates most with you—running the disciplined life or bringing your body under control? Can you relate to being side-tracked?

Exercise Fit Tip:

Schedule exercise in your calendar each week like you schedule any other important appointment you cannot break. Commit to your workout and healthy food prep as seriously as you do to your presentation at work or a meeting and you will make real progress.

God Can Orient Your Life

Tracy Hennes

"So here's what I want you to do, God helping you: Take your everyday, ordinary life—your sleeping, eating, going-to-work, and walking-around life—and place it before God as an offering. Embracing what God does for you is the best thing you can do for him. Don't become so well-adjusted to your culture that you fit into it without even thinking. Instead, fix your attention on God. You'll be changed from the inside out. Readily recognize what he wants from you, and quickly respond to it. Unlike the culture around you, always dragging you down to its level of immaturity, God brings the best out of you, develops well-formed maturity in you."

~Romans 12:1 (MSG)

In the midst of a long illness, I was forced to choose between the reputable career I had constructed my world around for the past eighteen years and my health. Reluctantly, I chose the latter, as I didn't feel I could manage the job and my current health situation. I was terrified and sad, but also excited about what I would get to do in this new life. The weeks and months after, I found myself riding waves of highs and lows and they were related to whether I began my day with "having to" get my kids ready for school versus "getting to" have that time with them. I needed to discover new joys in old tasks. I spent half of my life educating and serving children, but the winds had shifted and my sails were adjusted for a new course. There were days I praised Him and thanked God for the revision. It felt like I was going the direction He had been guiding me toward. But, to be honest, there were also days I felt lost and cried out, *'Really? What am I supposed to do now?'*

What are we to do when there is an instant shift in our lives and we find ourselves disoriented? We don't need to conform our calling to culture, nor do we need to orient our offerings to the ostentatious. God is especially honored and pleased when we submit even our simple steps and situations in a foundation of spirituality. We have an opportunity to honor Him with each of our actions, whether it is taking that extra second to smile and say hello, driving safely, preparing a meal, brushing our hair, exercising patience when waiting in line, or even doing the laundry. Our heavenly Father brings out the best in us, so let's recognize that and respond to daily life with spiritual maturity. When we live our lives in this manner, we become so firmly rooted in Him that we are not easily disoriented by whatever may come our way.

Father God, thank You for the lessons in Romans 12:1. Please help me to keep my attention on You so I that I can recognize the blessed opportunities provided in everyday situations. May my responses and all that I do honor all that You do for me.

Amen.

Exercise Your Faith

When you are thrown off-course, it's often small steps or a simple change in attitude that will help you to find your way. Imagine how differently your day would be if you'd approach tasks with a "get to" instead of "have to" attitude. What ordinary, everyday actions bring you satisfaction or help to keep you on-track? How could you respond to daily opportunities or offer your actions in a way that pleases your Heavenly Father?

 Exercise Fit Tip:

Remember to prioritize movement, not just the concept of exercise. Even on days you don't get a workout in, be sure you take a walk, stretch, stand, or dance! Your body was meant to move; enjoy it.

KEEP FIGHTING

Kathy Carter

"I have fought the good fight, I have finished the race, I have kept the faith."
~2 Timothy 4:7 (CSB)

Have you ever felt completely unfit for a challenge you thought you were ready for? That was me with motherhood. My husband and I were married for ten years before we decided to have children. For years, we only knew living for us. Around the time my biological clock started ticking, we both had an empty feeling in our hearts. We knew that was our calling to parenting. After two years of struggling and many disappointments, our baby was born. I read parenting books and took advice from everyone around me. Why did I feel so inadequate? Have you ever been told motherhood comes naturally? Not only did I feel like a failure, I developed an infection, a fever, and laryngitis.

The infection, mastitis, didn't allow me to nurse my son, making me feel like a failure. The fever drained my energy and, when he was upset, I couldn't even speak to him to soothe him because of my laryngitis. My physical limitations made me feel even more inadequate in my maternal duties.

Our little one was near colicky and I could not soothe him. I began doubting our parenthood decision.

I remember asking my older sister, "What year is the hardest?"

Her answer: "The year you are in."

Those were the truest words ever. Our son is now eighteen years old and I am grateful for the love and the struggles. He has tested our patience many times, but God knew fighting through the many battles of parenting would bring us closer to Him, while also sharing pure love and joy with our son!

2 Timothy 4:7 reminds Christians that we will face never-ending struggles against Satan's evil ways. We must keep the faith and put all of our trust in God who loves us. Many races are not all glory and effortless bliss and typically it is not the start that is hard, but the finish. Let us make up our minds to trust in the Lord through the tough times, so that we can look back at the end and say, *"I have fought the good fight and have finished the race."*

Dear God, Thank You for providing us all that we need. Thank You for reminding us that, even when we're feeling inadequate, You believe in us and our ability to meet the challenges before us. In Your name.

Amen.

Reflect on a time when you felt completely unfit for a challenge. What steps did you take to get through it? If you were to do it all over again, how would God lead you through?

_____
_____
_____
_____
_____
_____
_____
_____
_____
_____
_____
_____
_____
_____
_____
_____
_____
_____
_____
_____

 Exercise Fit Tip:

Whatever you tell yourself to get through a grueling workout, don't stop. Motivational self-talk can significantly help reduce the rate of perceived exertion (how loud your muscles are screaming), so you can go further for longer.

OUT OF THE GLOW AND INTO THE LIGHT

Luanne Nelson

"When Jesus spoke again to the people, he said, 'I am the light of the world. Whoever follows me will never walk in darkness, but will have the light of life.'"

~John 8:12 (NIV)

Rise and shine, Buttercup! Turn on the lights! Get going! It's going to be a great day! Sure, sometimes it would be fabulous during a cold wintery phase of life to burrow deeper into the soft, feathery, warm down comforter of life and sleep some more. There's too much to do - but it can wait. Clients to see - but another day. Friendships to nurture - but they'll understand. Prayers to say - but He already knows I love Him. The excuses. The clock ticks away. It is not waiting for me or for you or for anyone.

There are some things - like the truth - that just can't be put off any longer. It's time to get up. Time to show up. Do you sleep in the dark land of excuses?

The crowd turned a deaf ear to Jesus when He told them, *"I am the Light of the world."* The religious leaders were clueless what he meant because they were in a cold wintery phase of spiritual darkness. Even though they had the Law down pat, they didn't have the Light of Life. They didn't understand what Jesus was talking about at all. Many people follow false teachings to this day that lead to ruin. Jesus Christ is the true Light of Life.

We must exercise due diligence with His Word, submit ourselves to His teachings - even when we are too tired or too distracted. It's not enough to just see the glow from a distance, we have to train ourselves to seek His Light and follow it, exercise walking in it and learn how to live it. Discipline and discipleship. Rise and shine!

Dear Lord God, wake me up and teach me how to be Your disciple. Discipline me to get up, show up, lace up and turn on your Light of salvation in my life!

Amen.

Sometimes, it's easier to pull the covers over our head. It takes gumption to put our foot down on the floor and plow through the day anyway. Once our eyes adjust to the Light of the day, the going gets easier. What are the excuses you make most often to avoid getting the tasks at-hand completed? When we suit up and show up, Christ is with us every step of the way.

 **Exercise Fit Tip:**

After every bathroom break, do three to five jumping jacks to get the heart rate up and the oxygen pumping.

Transparency Allows Jesus To Shine Through

Marlene Dawson

> "Make this your common practice: Confess your sins to each other and pray for each other so that you can live together whole and healed. The prayer of a person living right with God is something powerful to be reckoned with."
>
> ~James 5:16 (MSG)

I was raised in a rough, abusive household. I had an active alcoholic father and an abused mother, who did her share of drinking. "Soft" is not a word anyone would use to describe me, except my oldest brother. I was loud, self-righteous, and always trying to prove I was worth your time and energy. It kept people away, allowing me to keep secrets that could never be exposed. When I became born again, God revealed my coping mechanisms were not valid for the Christian life. I wanted to change, but the shame was so deep I could not open up. When God decided to use me in His plans, I tentatively began sharing tiny pieces of my life. There was much rejection, but I knew I must go forward, or I would never be free.

In *James 5:16*, we are given the blueprint for Christian living: *confessing our sins to each other, and praying for each other, so we can be whole and healed.* While we are directed to share and pray together through our most difficult issues, we do not have to tell everything to everyone we meet. Testing the waters of trust and openness may be a new exercise, especially if there is any history of abuse.

Transparency is key to our being real and relatable. As we practice being open and honest with God, our trust in Him grows, which allows us to open up to others about the good, the bad, and the ugly of life. We start believing what God says about our identity in Christ: we are daughters of the King of Kings. We become transparent as we begin living life God's way. Transparency causes us to look more like Jesus, making us more effective vessels for His kingdom.

Lord, please show me what transparency looks like for me. I want to be available so you can use all of my life. Thank You, Lord.

Amen.

We choose how available we are for God's light to shine through. The more transparent we are, the more His love and healing power flows to others. What area is God revealing that He would like to soften or restore to help you become clear as glass? Do you have a trusted friend or counselor to help you walk through this process? Have you asked God to help? How did God answer?

Exercise Fit Tip:

Yoga is an incredible tool for staying healthy. Benefits are increased flexibility, increased muscle strength and tone, improved respiration, energy and vitality, balanced metabolism, weight reduction, cardio and circulatory health, improved athletic performance, and protection from injury.

MESSES TO MAGNIFICENCE THROUGH CHRIST

Luanne Nelson

"I can do all this through him who gives me strength."

~Philippians 4:13 (NIV)

Half of a lifetime ago, when I was in my thirties, my life was a total mess. If there was a bad relationship to get into, I was smack dab in the middle of it, saluting the strife. I had no idea how to get it right, so I went to a marriage counselor I found in the Yellow Pages. He told me my life sounded like a bad B-rated movie and suggested finding a quiet place under a tree or in a pew somewhere to talk to my Dad about the whole thing.

I didn't know it at the time; he meant God. I followed what I thought was his advice and found a great big tree to sit under. I had a long one-way talk about everything with my Dad who recently had died. I am certain, in retrospect, my Dad put me in touch with our Creator that day. I was sobbing. I missed my Dad. He was my mentor. At some point after this conversation under the tree, something clicked. I realized that my conversation with my earthly father was how I was supposed to be talking to God all along. It was the day I started doing everything in my life differently.

I no longer said, *'Father, God,'* I said, *'Dad, I need help.'*

I grew up and learned to approach my ultimate parent. I knew I was in good hands.

Change doesn't happen overnight. God is a patient Dad. When we exercise our bodies, we develop "muscle memory." The same thing happens when we exercise our Spirit. Sometimes quickly, sometimes slowly we change from the inside out. He gives us just the right amount of strength and clarity we need at every given moment. He knows exactly what we need and He never fails us.

Dear Almighty Father, please give me the courage to get in the race. I know You will give the me strength I need to get to the finish line where You and my Dad will be waiting for me.

Amen.

Sometimes we feel like giving up; life gets rough and we get tired. People disappoint us; we disappoint ourselves. This is where Jesus Christ comes in and never fails us. *("Praise the Lord! He is good. God's love never fails." Psalm 136:1 NIV)* All we have to do is flex our spiritual muscles and ask for help. He's right there with us. It's humbling and glorious at the same time. Take a moment to remember the times you felt like giving up but then realized you were not alone. Sometimes He gives us the strength we need in places we'd never think of looking. Who has God sent into your life to give you a hand?

_____
_____
_____
_____
_____
_____
_____
_____
_____
_____
_____
_____
_____
_____
_____
_____
_____

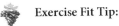 **Exercise Fit Tip:**

The minimum amount of exercise an adult needs is walking four to five miles each day.

The Great and Uncomfortable Commission

Marlene Dawson

> "Then Jesus came to them and said, 'All authority in heaven and on earth has been given to me. Therefore go and make disciples of all nations, baptizing them in the name of the Father, and of the Son, and of the Holy Spirit, and teaching them to obey everything I have commanded you. And surely I am with you always, to the very end of the age.'"
>
> ~Matthew 28:18-20 (NIV)

A number of years ago, my best friend became pregnant. The father was not around, and she decided abortion was her only option. I said everything I could to dissuade her, but she was determined. My prayers filled with tears as the appointment drew near, until I heard Holy Spirit whisper, *'Offer to go along with her.'*

I know that voice well, so I made the offer. She called the morning of her appointment saying she changed her mind. My hopes and joy were dashed as she continued, "I do not want you to come."

I cried out to God, *'Lord, only You can stop this!'*

When she called later, I did not expect her to scream, "They wouldn't let me have the abortion! They said I'm too far along!" Then she slammed the phone down.

I continued praying for and trying to contact her, and she finally agreed to meet for coffee. God restored our relationship and gifted my friend with the relationship she would have with her son. She is still one of my dearest friends and I didn't have to compromise God's truth to maintain our friendship.

How scary is it when God asks you to step out of your comfort zone for His purposes? Matthew 28:18-20 is called the Great Commission, when Jesus instructed His disciples to take the gospel to every nation. It's our turn to take God's love, acceptance, and forgiveness to our family, friends, and neighbors. Many people think it is difficult or scary to share this good news, but the Great Commission includes Jesus' promise that He will be with us each step of the way. When we believe Jesus is always with us, we can embrace the lost and needy. We get to tell others how God created space for a relationship with us, and that He wants to have a loving relationship with them as well.

Father God, sometimes it is difficult to share my faith. Please give me courage to live my life so others desire to know You. Thank You, Lord.

Amen.

Exercise Your Faith

Living in God's love gives us opportunities to tell others how much He loves them. Think of a time when God directed you to speak to a friend or neighbor. If you were you scared, in what ways does knowing that Jesus always has your back make a difference? How did you step out and embrace the opportunity?

_____
_____
_____
_____
_____
_____
_____
_____
_____
_____
_____
_____
_____
_____
_____
_____
_____
_____
_____
_____

 Exercise Fit Tip:

Try something new. Working out doesn't have to be the gym. You can go for a hike, take a tennis lesson, or even do a dance class. Find out what is fun for you so you will be consistent while doing something that makes you smile.

RIDING ON GOD'S BACK

Susan Brozek

> "Trust in the LORD with all your heart and lean not on your own understanding; in all your ways acknowledge Him, and He shall direct your paths."
>
> ~Proverbs 3:5-6 (NKJV)

Have you ever just wished you could know what would happen tomorrow . . . next week . . . a month from now? Maybe even five years from now? I am one of those people who loves to be able to know what the big picture is. I like to be able to figure everything out, and "peek around the corner." I was that child who always asked, *'Why?'*

While why questions now help me tremendously in my private psychotherapy practice since I love to get to the root of issues, and not just treat symptoms . . . when it comes to God's plan for my life, this why tendency can become a potential stumbling block! I have needed to accept that God is not going to show me the full planned timeline of my life, neatly laid out well in advance. And deep down, I know that this would not be beneficial to me; we are not meant to possess that type of knowledge for our own lives. What would be the purpose of "trusting in the Lord with all of our heart" if life operated this way?

The Hebrew word for "trust" means to literally "roll onto the back" of someone. In the context of this passage, we are being asked to roll ourselves onto God's back! When someone is carrying you on his back, your feet are off the ground and you merely lean your weight onto the One who carries you. What a beautiful picture of what the Lord asks us to do! And He tells us that when we do so and acknowledge Him in all our ways, He Himself will direct our paths.

We don't have to figure everything out years in advance and plan our own steps, or make our own way. God does the heavy lifting and we are simply along for the ride...an amazingly and thoughtfully planned ride which gives God all the glory due His Name!

Dear Abba Father, help us to trust You more. Since our understanding is finite, help us to not lean on it...but rather lean on Your infinite understanding and good plans and purposes for our lives. Lord, You know full well what You are doing. Enable us to submit to You and Your work.

Amen.

Exercise Your Faith

Think of circumstances you may be going through for which you are currently relying on your own understanding, instead of trusting in God and His direction. What would change in your life if you were to "roll yourself onto God's back" and allow him to carry you and steer you down the path of His choosing? What would need to happen for you to yield to His wisdom, without knowing what the future holds?

_____
_____
_____
_____
_____
_____
_____
_____
_____
_____
_____
_____
_____
_____
_____
_____
_____
_____
_____
_____

 **Exercise Fit Tip:**

Core and back exercises greatly diminish or eliminate back pain.

GOD'S STRENGTH MOVES THROUGH OUR WEAKNESSES

Danelle Skinner

> "My strength comes into its own in your weakness. Once I heard that, I was glad to let it happen. I quit focusing on the handicap and began appreciating the gift."
>
> ~2 Corinthians 12:9 (MSG)

Often, we forget this promise and that's exactly where Satan wants us, focused on our weaknesses. Struggling to move forward, exercising our faith. The word "faith" is used over 200 times in the New Testament and, almost every time it is used, it relates to a person's action. Faith is an action. We could sit on our couches all day believing we could run a marathon, but it takes faith in our ability to get up and run.

Unlike Satan, God does not want us focused on our weaknesses. He wants us focused on His strengths, ability, and care for us. The stronger we believe God is, the more willing we will be to move forward, trusting He will equip us to do whatever He has called us to do. *"May he equip you with all you need for doing His will. May he produce in you, through the power of Jesus Christ, every good thing that is pleasing to Him. All glory to Him forever and ever! Amen."* (Hebrews 13:21 NIV)

I am currently experiencing this promise. I highly disliked English class in school and had to attend special education classes to learn how to read. I would have never fathomed becoming a writer. Yet, my weaknesses didn't matter to God. He laid it on my heart to do this devotional and—although I thought I was not equipped for His calling—it quickly became clear: He called me to write. He had already been orchestrating this theme in all areas of my life – At church, Bible study, my personal devotions, a class I'm taking with my son, our women's retreat, and my personal life have all been focused on this exact topic! topic. He was surrounding me by it, equipping me little by little to do what He was getting me ready to do. As I sought Him daily, His strengths have written these devotions regardless of my weaknesses!

Seeing the Lord work through our weaknesses has become my all-time favorite thing! If I would have focused on my weaknesses, Satan would have celebrated.

If God has called you to *Exercise Your Faith*, He will equip you to do it. So, let's stop focusing on our weaknesses, handicaps, and shortcomings. Let's focus our attention on receiving the gift of God's strength.

God thank You for moving Your strength through my weaknesses. Lord, help me to Exercise My Faith by taking action.

Amen

Exercise Your Faith

Our action or inaction tells us a lot about what we believe to be true about God's strength, faithfulness, and ability. In which of your weaknesses does God want to be your strength? What type of action does God want you to take in spite of your weakness, so that He can be strong for you?

_____

 Exercise Fit Tip:

Think of strength training as your main dish and cardio as your side!

STAND FIRM

Teresa Kliner

> "Therefore put on the full armor of God, so that when the day of evil comes you may be able to stand your ground and after you have done everything to stand. Stand firm with the belt of truth buckled around your waist, with the breastplate of righteousness in place, and your feet fitted with the readiness that comes from the gospel of peace."
>
> ~Ephesians 6:13-15 (NIV)

I love thinking through the armor of God and visualizing putting on each piece. In *Kill the Spider: Getting Rid of What's Really Holding You Back* by Carlos Whittaker, he teaches about how everything is attached to the belt of truth. As with a police officer, everything is right at the waist for easy access to what they need to protect them from anything that comes at them.

Also true with the armor of God, everything gets fastened to the truth of God's Word, to God himself as the truth and He (the truth) will set us free. The key is knowing the truth. If I am not constantly reaching for God's truth, I end up giving in to the lies and allowing them to win.

I am defenseless without my armor. However, we can safeguard against the enemy's attacks. We can put on the whole armor so we can stand our ground, but we don't have to fight. Typically, when we think about being all dressed in armor, we think of a soldier going to battle. The great news is that we don't have to go to battle to fight. We have to put on the armor and then stand . . . stand firm.

God has already won the battle for us. We are already free. We just need the armor for protection against the enemy that comes to kill, steal, and destroy. If we are geared up we don't need to know how to fight. We just need to know how to stand. We will take arrows. We will see battle. It's not ours to fight. We must only stand firm.

Lord, help me to know Your truth and to do the daily discipline of putting on the armor, so that when the arrows come—I can stand firm. Thank You that You love us so much and that You have won this battle. Help us to have the strength to stand firm.

Amen.

Exercise Your Faith

We all struggle. The Bible tells us it will happen. Thankfully we have a safeguard against our struggles. How can you gear up for battle? How can you make sure you are grounded in the truth of God's Word and not your own thoughts? What can you do today to start the discipline you will need to stand firm?

___

Exercise Fit Tip:

Stand or walk while tiptoeing as you get dressed each morning. This posture works the core and leg muscles and helps increase balance.

PRODUCTIVE WAITING

Lisa Danegelis

"But those who wait on the Lord shall renew their strength. They shall mount up with wings like eagles, they shall run and not grow weary, they shall walk and not faint."

~Isaiah 40:31 (NKJV)

Run? Me run? I knew it was God's voice, I had learned to sense it long ago. But surely He was mistaken this time!

My son had been in the Surgical Intensive Care Unit (S.I.C.U) for weeks and would soon spend months in a rehab center with four shattered limbs and a brain injury following a motorcycle accident. I was feeling helpless, unable to converse normally with him or even hold his hand. The waiting was exhausting. God knew my frustration and desire to do something that felt productive. But run? I was not a runner and had no desire to start, but those nagging words persisted . . . so I ran.

I ran for my son. I ran because he couldn't. I taped his picture and "running our race" Bible verses on my treadmill. I pleaded, praised, and trusted day after day as I ran. God knew what I needed. He stepped in and gave me a physical and emotional outlet for my pain as my son slowly healed. I was able to show him the verse-and-picture-plastered treadmill recently. It was a joy to see him take his first steps and I believe, as we wait on the Lord, he will also run again!

We often think of waiting as passive. We see life streaming by us and we are unable to jump in and be a part of it. Our time waiting on Him can be productive. We can choose to settle our souls before Him and pray and praise. We can learn to sense His beauty in stillness and *Exercise Our Faith* by simple trust.

Did you notice in the verse above that the walking and running come after the waiting? Find solace in the waiting . . . until God tells you to run.

Father, as I wait on You, help me to rest in simple trust. Quiet my busy mind and give me peace.

Amen.

Exercise Your Faith

Do you have a situation in your life that is at a standstill? Are you frustrated and even desperate to "make something happen?" Journal about your frustrations and ask God if there is anything productive you can do while you wait. Look up several verses on waiting in a concordance and meditate on them, asking for wisdom you could apply to your situation.

Exercise Fit Tip:

While sitting, lift the heels and just have the balls of your feet on the ground. This will give the muscles in the calves some work to do. Lift and hold your legs for an additional workout while you sit.

WHERE'S YOUR FOCUS

Teresa Kliner

"But seek first his kingdom and his righteousness and all these things will be given to you as well."

~ Matthew 6:33 (NIV)

My daughter and I went for a walk and, as we walked, I started showing her all of my favorite trees as they were changing colors and dropping their leaves. We both were in awe of the same tree. With the way the sun hit it, it appeared to be the prettiest, brightest gold I'd ever seen. We both took pictures of it and failed miserably at capturing its true, raw beauty. My daughter explained to me that when you take a picture without special focusing capabilities, the camera is focusing on the "whole" picture . . . the tree plus all of its surroundings. Therefore, you don't get the focused beauty of just the tree. However, our eyesight is able to focus only on the tree. When we looked at the tree, the surroundings faded away and the tree was even more brilliant.

As we walked I thought, *'Wow!'* Isn't that so true about life. What we focus on is what we see clearly. The rest of life fades away and isn't as important or as bright as what we are focusing on. The question is . . . where is the focus? If the focus is on our job, then our surroundings (our family, our health, etc.) fade away into the background.

Our jobs don't feed into our surroundings; however, God does.

He says if we seek and focus on His kingdom and righteousness all these things will be given to you as well. All these things in the picture that are faded into the background will be taken care of, too. You don't have to focus and worry about each one individually. We just need to focus on one thing, Him, and the rest will fall into place. He will guide us on the rest.

Lord, help me to seek You today, allow the worries of life to fade into the background and help me focus on You alone!

Amen.

Exercise Your Faith

Today all we have to do is Seek Him! Give God our attention and He will help us with all the other demands of life. Take some time to evaluate where your focus is today? What is something you could implement into your daily routine to continuously seek Him first?

Exercise Fit Tip:

Who you choose to surround yourself with is a direct reflection of how you see yourself. If you want to be fit, successful, and healthier, surround yourself with people who model this in their own lives and who will support you in your goals.

WHAT DO YOU MAGNIFY?

Kathy Thorsen

> "My child, pay attention to what I say. Listen carefully to my words. Don't lose sight of them. Let them penetrate deep into your heart, for they bring life to those who find them, and healing to their whole body. Guard your heart above all else, for it determines the course of your life."
>
> ~Proverbs 4:20-23 (NLT)

The complex rhythms of the heart or Heart Rate Variability (HRV), as studied by the Heartmath[1] Institute, are not only a source of life but also wisdom into the mental, emotional and relational aspects that sustain humanity. Biofeedback technology such as that developed by the Heartmath Institute utilizes personal devices to measure heart coherence, the patterns of the heart as they relate to the function of other physiological systems like the respiratory and neurological systems. When we experience stress, anger or sadness heart coherence is low reflecting a chaotic state. In positive emotional states, the heart rhythms become orderly and coherence among systems increases, thus health is improved.

In our modern society where everything is connected through technology, it is easy to be distracted and direct our attention to the latest fad, gossip, or accomplishments, woes and slander posted on social media or in the cloud. I find it difficult as an adult to determine how much time I should spend keeping up with the information that floods my multiple "receivers" and how to mitigate stress. The science of Heartmath has shown that gratitude and love, the very things God instructs in His Word, bring one's heartbeats into coherence. Mindfully focusing on scripture circulates God's Word throughout our hearts and directs us to a righteous life . . . one filled with gratitude and love.

The instructions for our lives are clearly written in the scripture. All we have to do is take the time to remove the distractions so we can read, quietly reflect on, and carefully listen to His "text" messages. The more we pay attention to His words found imbedded even in modern technology as well as numerous non-electronic sources, the deeper it will penetrate our heart and mind.

It is no coincidence that scientific research has once again has substantiated God's Word. The Heartmath research shows that positive emotions result in a healing effect on the entire body, as well as improved perception, emotional resilience, and performance. God's Word is natural medicine!

Thank You, God, for Your words of everlasting life. Help me to set aside distractions so that I may replenish my mind and heart with these life-supporting treasures that will be shared with all whom I meet.   *Amen.*

---

[1] https://www.heartmath.com

How often do you set aside a time of solace in your day to renew your thoughts with God's Word? What would need to happen for you to spend one percent of your day, just fifteen minutes, in prayer to allow our Creator to bring coherence to your heart?

 Exercise Fit Tip:

Twice a week, instead of going at a steady pace for thirty minutes, go easy for three minutes and hard for one minute. Repeat this pattern five to six times; you'll have a new workout and a calorie burning machine!

Joyful Thanksgiving Releases The Promise

Kimberly Joy Krueger

"Thanksgiving will come out of them, a sound of celebration. I will multiply them, and they will not decrease; I will honor them, and they will not be insignificant."

~Jeremiah 30:19 (NIV)

My business wasn't growing fast enough. I wanted to reach more women with God's message of extraordinary living. His whispers told me He was going to multiply my efforts any minute and I would see that longed-for harvest. Yet, there was very little movement. Maybe some addition here and there, but no multiplication that I could see. My discouragement was about to cross over to full-on whining when some divine wisdom appeared in my inbox. It said: "Ask the Lord to give you a strategy to recover it all."

When I read that message, I immediately knew that the Lord was going to tell me how to recover His promise to multiply my reach. So . . . I asked . . . and He answered in the form of Jeremiah 30:18-22. God's promise to multiply and not decrease His people jumped off the page! I can be slow at times, but I picked up on this one pretty fast. He was confirming His promise to me once again!

But what about a strategy? Was there really something I could do to reap a multiplied harvest? As I read it again, I saw that, while God was doing many things in this passage, His people were doing only one: giving thanks! And, not just politely, but with a sound of celebration! It was like Heaven was telling me, *'Oh, things aren't moving? Your efforts aren't being multiplied? Well, around here, that calls for a party! Celebrate today as if it's already happened!'*

God's ways are not our ways, so it shouldn't surprise us that when we feel furthest from the promise and are the least thankful, it is joyful thanksgiving that releases that promise. I wanted my Promise released! Do you know how silly it feels jumping up and down in your kitchen thanking God for something that hasn't even happened yet? I do! Because He gave me a strategy, no—an opportunity—to reap my harvest, and I wasn't going to miss it!

Wonderful Father, I thank You for fulfilling the promises You have made me! I celebrate in advance, the abundant harvest my life will one day produce to bring You glory! It will happen! Hallelujah!

Amen.

It took faith for me to celebrate something I'd only ever seen in my imagination. What is something God has promised you that you have only seen in mind's eye? Would you be willing to "reap your harvest" by celebrating like it has already come to pass? If so, what would your celebration look like? What does your prayer of joyful thanksgiving sound like? (Now do it!)

Exercise Fit Tip:

Circuit-style workouts supercharge your metabolism and help you shed pounds. By getting your heart rate up and working each muscle group, you can create a lean and sleek physique.

COURAGEOUS FAITH

Tracy Hennes

"So be strong and courageous! Do not be afraid and do not panic before them. For the Lord your God will personally go ahead of you. He will neither fail you nor abandon you."

~Deuteronomy 31:6 (NLT)

Have you ever aimed at a health goal and then found yourself paralyzed by the fear of failure? Maybe you've longed to kick your sugar habit? Eat healthier? Run? Complete a thirty-day challenge? Join a yoga class? Maybe you've attempted to lose weight and failed?

When it comes to exercise, I have an intense case of "gym-timidation"; a paralyzing fear of looking like a fool, or worse, a failure. I can recall a few times when I've joined a gym and then don't use the membership. Month after month I pay my dues, but there's a voice that convinces me I can't go. I step foot in the door a few times and meet the trainer to take the "newbie tour." I wander into a group fitness class and awkwardly try to keep pace with the instructor. I may even intend to work out at home, but when I hit a "too busy" week, I give in to defeat and resign from my resolve.

Have you ever let fear win? Has fear kept you from trying something new? Skipped out on a difficult conversation? Took a "pass" on visiting an unfamiliar place or going it alone? What are we afraid of? Acceptance? Being ourselves?

While we may abandon our goal because of fear, God does not abandon us. We may feel like a failure, but He does not fail us. If we are compelled toward completion, then we are called to not give in to panic. Be strong. God gives us power and strength, not fear, for all that we are called to. Remember, the King of all Creation cares so much about our well-being that he "personally" goes ahead of us!

Exercise Your Faith in courage and push toward that goal. After all, the greatest "coach" of all time is leading the way!

God, thank You for walking before me so that I can be courageous, knowing You will never abandon me. Help me, Lord, to not give in to my fears or the voice of the enemy so that I can stay the course to achieve the goals that honor and glorify You.

Amen.

When was the last time you felt too intimidated to finish because you were afraid of failure or judgment from others? Knowing that God is with you always, leading the way, what could you do to push past the fear and glorify His commitment to you?

_____
_____
_____
_____
_____
_____
_____
_____
_____
_____
_____
_____
_____
_____
_____
_____
_____
_____

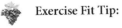 **Exercise Fit Tip:**

A comprehensive exercise regime includes regular sessions of cardio, strength-training and stretching.

HE WRAPS US IN STRENGTH

Margaret Bentham-Moe

"She wraps herself in strength, might and power in all her works."

~Proverbs 31:17 (TPT)

A virtuous woman is proactive, motivated, and lives with a sense of purpose. One might be tempted to think she's some sort of superwoman, endowed with special powers, atypical of "real" women, when—in fact—she's the Bible's blueprint for all women who submit their lives to God. Her attributes are a natural outcome from spending time with Abba, so it's available to all of us. It wouldn't be possible for this woman to wrap herself in strength had she not gotten it from the Lord whose joy is our strength.

On busy days, I've attempted to get all items on my bucket list completed: Get the family out the door with a well-balanced meal. Get outside and water all my plants. Run errands. Finish the laundry. Clean the cupboards. Fix that shelf that's been on the checklist forever! Organize! Though I start early, there was little to show for my effort. I work hard all day and don't finish! Whenever this happened my only reward was frustration. Have you ever had days like those?

On the other hand, when I put first things first and spend time with the Lord, I wonder *'how in the world did I accomplish so much today?'* Aren't those the best days?

I've found that, to live successfully each day, I too must first wrap myself with the strength that only our God gives. Many brides know that, to preserve a wedding dress, you wrap it in blue, so that it isn't affected by the ultraviolet rays and won't get discolored or damaged. It's precious and should be protected. When we wrap something up, it's no longer affected by outside influences and can only interact with what's on the inside of the package. This is what happens when we daily allow our loving Heavenly Father to wrap us up in His love and wisdom.

If we wrap ourselves in the Word of God, we are protected from worldly elements. Our very atmosphere changes; we're strengthened inwardly and we also become virtuous women, blessed with might and power to accomplish any task.

Abba, Father, in You alone we find strength, might, and power. Help us to be consistent in seeking You daily and to yield ourselves to the precious Holy Spirit, our Helper, so that our lives would bring praise and glory to You. In the mighty name of Jesus, our Lord and Savior.

Amen.

Isn't it wonderful that God has equipped us to live effectively through His strength? How can you more effectively wrap yourself in the attributes God has in store for you? What does seeking Him more and more look like for you?

_____
_____
_____
_____
_____
_____
_____
_____
_____
_____
_____
_____
_____
_____
_____
_____
_____
_____
_____
_____

 Exercise Fit Tip:

Add some muscle-building activities to your weekly workout using free weights, bands, or just simply your own body weight with pushups, planks, and squats.

YOU WILL NOT BE SWEPT AWAY OR SET ABLAZE

Danelle Skinner

"When you pass through the waters, I will be with you; and when you pass through the rivers, they will not sweep over you. When you walk through the fire, you will not be burned; the flames will not set you ablaze."

~Isaiah 43:2 (NIV)

What does life look like when you feel like you're stuck in the middle of a huge rain storm? The clouds are rumbling, dark and fierce. Rivers are crashing. Powerlines are going down starting fires everywhere. Do you feel like the waters from the storm might sweep over you or like everything might go up in flames? Not long ago, I felt like I was barely holding my head above water and everything around me was on fire, but the waters never swept over me and I was not set ablaze. He never left even when I was barely above water and surrounded by fire.

I'm going to say what no mom thinks they can or should say. I hated being a housewife and mom and I hated myself for hating being a mom. I completely lost my worldly identity as I knew it. Meanwhile, I was physically ill with what turned out to be mold toxicity and because this occurred even while pregnant, my children also have issues. I was tired, oh so tired! I was toxic in body, mind, and spirit. I had already seen several different doctors looking for answers. Then one day the weight of the guilt I felt surrounding motherhood became so heavy I fell to my knees and begged God for help. *"Lord, please help me!! I can't carry the weight of this anymore. It's drowning me. Please help me be completely filled by being a mom. Please heal me or lead me to healing Lord! Amen."* In the middle of my storm, I ran toward Jesus. I knew He was my only way out. I did not have the strength, the will or the tools to make it out of the storm alive without Him!

The day after my prayer, I met a new friend. She had been through many of my same struggles. She walked beside me through my struggles in mind, body, and soul. God put the right people into my life to weather my storm. My mind is no longer toxic. My body is overcoming toxicity. I can lay by my child and see and feel love with a sense of peace. My spirit is completely filled by being a daughter of the Lord.

What do you do when life is a big storm? Do you stop walking toward Jesus completely and start clinging to some worldly thing you have chosen to put your faith into? Do you start running toward Him, knowing He is the only thing that can withstand life's storms without being swept away by the waters or burned by the flames? God knows us, He cares for us, and He never leaves us. He will not let us be swept away or set ablaze. Therefore, in the storms of life, we must make the intentional choice to set our eyes on Jesus and run toward Him. He is the only one strong enough to withstand, control, and protect us from the storm!

Dear God, thank You for never leaving me, even in the midst of my storms. Thank You for protecting me from being swept away or set ablaze. *Amen.*

Exercise Your Faith

We run toward Jesus, because He is strong enough to withstand the storm and the fire. What storm or fire are you trying to fend off these days? Have you proven strong enough on your own? If not, write a prayer telling God that you are running toward Him instead. Ask Him how to lean on His strength to save you.

_____
_____
_____
_____
_____
_____
_____
_____
_____
_____
_____
_____
_____
_____
_____
_____
_____
_____

 **Exercise Fit Tip:**

Park in the spot that's furthest away from the entrances. This will increase your daily steps.

Godfidence Is A Glorious Reward!

Rebecca Grambort

"Do not, therefore, fling away your [fearless] confidence, for it has a glorious and great reward. For you have need of patient endurance [to bear up under difficult circumstances without compromising], so that when you have carried out the will of God, you may receive and enjoy to the full what is promised."

~Hebrews 10:35-36 (AMP)

Years ago, I would find it perplexing that God would deliver this word in command form "....*DO NOT fling away your [fearless] confidence....*" I wanted to argue with Him that I couldn't fling away something that I didn't even possess! I was the prize-owner of insecurity and fearfulness at best. Any confidence that I did have lay inside of my self-induced labels such as wife and mother. Then, after the tragic death of my spouse, that confidence was completely compromised. My other options of escaping my new reality were less than appealing, and so bearing-up-under would become my new way of life. My anguish led me to place my only hope in Jesus. Because of my desperation, I went to great lengths to seek Him and it would bring me a great and glorious reward.

Knowing Him!

He not only revealed to me who He was, but also revealed who I was and who I was created to be! It took time and effort, but I eventually became the proud owner of a confidence that could not be flung away.

What I learned is that there is a difference between confidence that is found in self and confidence that is found in Him. Unshakable confidence is knowing who He is and knowing who you are in Christ. Once these two truths are revealed to you and they become rooted into your spirit, it becomes easier to patiently endure while you wait for Him and carry out His will for your life! While you wait – DO NOT - throw away your Godfidence! It has a great and glorious reward!

Heavenly Father; Help me to confidently trust that You are who You say You are so that I can patiently endure. I know that my fearless confidence will have a great and glorious reward!

Amen.

Exercise Your Faith

Have you ever done core strengthening exercises? Core muscles stabilize and support your entire body. Like this, confidence is the core muscle that supports and stabilizes your whole spiritual being. This helps us to patiently endure difficult seasons. What would your life look like if you had confidence? Build your core by asking God who He is, and then who you are. Write what you hear from Him below. Let this be your confidence!

_____
_____
_____
_____
_____
_____
_____
_____
_____
_____
_____
_____
_____
_____
_____
_____
_____
_____

Exercise Fit Tip:

You don't have to work out for an hour every time you hit the gym. Do as much as you can but do something. Just stay consistent and learn to build the healthy pattern. Showing up is half the battle!

NOW FAITH!

Candice Moe

"NOW FAITH IS the substance of things hoped for, the evidence of things not seen. For by it the elders obtained a good report."

~Hebrews 11:1-2 (NRV)

"The fundamental fact of existence is that this Trust in God, this Faith, is the firm foundation under everything that makes life worth living. It's our handle on what we can't see. The Act-of-Faith is what distinguished our ancestors, set them above the crowd. By Faith, we see the world called into existence by God's Word, what we see created by what we don't see." (Hebrews 11:1-3 MSG) As a child of God, is your endeavor to please Abba? Does your heart beat to make His sing? Hopefully you're not forgoing all His benefits (Psalm 103:2). A Father is intrinsically, a provider. Your Heavenly Father is no exception. He's greatly esteemed when you receive.

"...Jesus, tired from the long walk, sat wearily beside the well about noontime. Soon a Samaritan woman came to draw water, and Jesus said to her, 'Please give Me a drink.'...The woman was surprised, for Jews refuse to have anything to do with Samaritans. She said to Jesus, 'You are a Jew, and I am a Samaritan woman. Why are You asking me for a drink?' Jesus replied, 'If you only knew the Gift God has for you and Who you are speaking to, you would ask Me, and I would give you Living Water.'" (John 4:6-7, 9-10 NLT)

"It is your Father's good pleasure to give you the Kingdom." (Luke 12:32 NLT) Children aren't their own custodians as the onus rests entirely upon parents. Generally, lavishly attired parents, don't parade scantily clad children or feed them meager rations. Yet, some accept this distortion about Abba.

Could it be we've been 'believing' wrong? Now Faith is substance . . . tangible! Jesus pronounced in *Mark 11:24 (TPT)*, "This is the reason I urge you to boldly BELIEVE for whatever you ask for in prayer—BELIEVE that you have received it and it WILL be yours."

Faith is not something you can store up, like electricity it is available only in the continuous now.

Actions unveil beliefs! Core beliefs are unaffected by time and circumstance, believing Jesus, must be unwavering . . . relentless! Neither negative medical findings, financial difficulties, nor the climate of world affairs will supersede God's Word. One medical report exists for a child of God: Isaiah 53:5. One financial statement: Deuteronomy 8:18, one media correspondence: Revelation 12:11!

Jesus help me receive Your Word as final authority in my life. Holy Spirit I rely on You. Remind me of truths read daily in Your Word.

Amen.

Exercise Your Faith

What's your default when unbiblical communications loom? Without faith, it is impossible to please God. What is something that He has been telling you that you can choose to wholeheartedly receive and believe today? What steps will you take so that you "Now Faith" may arise? Write those steps down and remind yourself of them by reading them often.

_____

 Exercise Fit Tip:

After exercise, our muscles can be depleted and thirsty for nutrition. Protein is an essential building block for muscle fibers to be able to rebuild after being worked.

JOY IS A KNOWING

Lisa Danegelis

> "Though the fig tree may not blossom, nor fruit be on the vine. Though the labor of the olive tree may fail, and the fields yield no food. Though the flock may be cut off from the fold and there be no herd in the stalls. Yet will I rejoice in the Lord. I will joy in the God of my salvation."
>
> ~Habakkuk 3: 17-18 (NKJV)

I walked through the field with a consuming ache in my soul, carrying a cross crafted from twigs and a piece of paper scribbled with the letters: W-H-Y. I dug a hole, buried the paper, and stuck the cross in the "grave." I was outwardly representing my inward spiritual surrender. I had been released from another inpatient stay at a mental health facility . . . one of seven I endured over the course of seven years. A very stressful time had thrown me head first into the mental health arena of diagnosis and drugging. I had been reduced to what felt like quivering raw flesh. For years, I had been begging God for answers to my mental, physical, and emotional decline. *'Why?'* was my constant refrain, yet God was silent. So I buried my why for good. I stopped searching for answers in the Bible and devotionals. I stopped repenting, rebuking, and fasting. I nearly stopped praying.

Doing nothing became the hardest thing this overachiever ever did.

I wrote lists as in Habakkuk: Even though_____ , yet will I praise You. I filled in the blank over and over, surrendering my heartaches and questions. I sat in stillness with Him and, over time, I wrote this in my journal, "God and I became easy." He captured my heart again. I learned that joy can always be available for me when I move my focus from my struggles to God's love.

It is easy to confuse joy and happiness. Happiness depends on something. Joy depends on someone. This crazy world will always let us down. Relationships crumble, health declines, and material possessions lose their luster. Joy doesn't have to be a feeling, it can be a knowing. It is a gift of the Holy Spirit to be embraced, practiced, and celebrated. This world will always disappoint.

When happiness is scarce, we can always find joy in the truths of God's Word.

Father, help me to surrender my whys and to rejoice in the joy of my salvation.

Amen.

Exercise Your Faith

Use this space to journal an *"Even though,_____, yet will I praise You"* list. Surrender your current obstacles, questions, and future fears on the blank line. Visualize yourself handing each to God and feel the peace of knowing that whatever your remaining years hold, God will be more than enough.

Exercise Fit Tip:

Tense your muscles while in elevators, on moving sidewalks, or on escalators to help engage them and encourage toning.

Finish By Faith

Candice Moe

"Another example is Rahab. She was a prostitute, but she was made right with God by something she did. She helped those who were spying for God's people. She welcomed them into her home and helped them escape by a different road. A person's body that does not have a spirit is dead. It is the same with faith— faith that does nothing is dead!"

~James 2:25-26 (ERV)

Motionless! Not a very impressive word. Like muscle, faith requires activity for development. Imagine an egg in a frying pan – uncracked, unbeaten, and yet full of delicious potential. Potential is a good initiator, but it is action that achieves results.

Faith is believing God. Works is obedience exercised in response to Faith. Hearing Abba's Voice is a prestige afforded every believer. The Father continuously speaks to your spirit and through His Word. *You were saved by Grace through Faith for Good works. (Ephesians 2:8-10)* Merely believing in Jesus does not differentiate a saint from a sinner, even Satan believes, yet he cowers, afraid of your Heavenly Father (James 2:19) and of Christ in you . . . the Hope of Glory. (Colossians 1:27)

Peradventure you're currently believing The Father for restoration of your marriage, health, or finances. Have you been actuated by the Word of God or by the Holy Spirit's promptings to step out and do? Whether He's leading you to forgive, sow financial seed, volunteer at your local hospice or spend more time reading the Bible, it behooves implementation. Finish by faith! Walking in obedience is pivotal for fruitfulness, spawning miracles, signs, and wonders.

Let us garner truth from a few faith pioneers:

1. It was by faith that Noah finished building a large boat to save his family from the flood. He obeyed God, who warned him about things that had never happened before. By his faith Noah condemned the rest of the world, and he received the righteousness that comes by faith.
2. It was by faith that Abraham obeyed when God called him to leave home and go to another land that God would give him as his inheritance. He went without knowing where he was going.
3. It was by faith that Abraham offered Isaac as a sacrifice when God was testing him. Abraham, who had received God's promises, was ready to sacrifice his only son, Isaac, even though God had told him, "Isaac is the son through whom your descendants will be counted." Abraham reasoned that if Isaac died, God was able to bring him back to life again. And in a sense, Abraham did receive his son back from the dead.
4. It is by faith that you will have all of your needs and your Godly desires met. (2 Peter 1:3 NLT)

Thank You Jesus for Grace to walk out my faith. I trust Your guidance, even into the unfamiliar, knowing You love me and Your plans for my life are amazing. Amen.

Exercise Your Faith

Write down the area or areas you have asked Abba to restore in your life. Then ask Him what steps . . . what actions . . . He is asking you to take to reflect your faith. Listen for His still, small voice, imagine what needs and desires God will meet when you trust your faith, and share what God is promising you in your journal below.

_____
_____
_____
_____
_____
_____
_____
_____
_____
_____
_____
_____
_____
_____
_____
_____
_____
_____
_____
_____

Exercise Fit Tip:

After a workout, use a foam roller to gently glide along tired muscles to help push out toxins and lactic acid buildup.

Rest Of God

*The **Rest of God** is just as important for our souls as sleep is for our bodies.*

Just as the body needs rest from activity, thought, and work, so our minds and hearts need rest from the cares of this life.

The Rest of God is a place, like sleep, whereby we are rejuvenated, refreshed, and restored for what the day requires of us. The Rest of God is a place of peace, even in the midst of a storm. It is a safe haven and it is available to every believer.

The Word of God has strong words to say about entering into the Rest that God provides, but sadly, few learn to do so.

It is our prayer that these devotionals will inspire you to lay your cares at the feet of Jesus and enter into His peaceful rest. May you choose to trust completely in Him to meet all of your needs and to finish the good work He began in you.

May you rest fully in His arms of love!

Rest Is In The Design

Jane Guffy

"And he said to them, "The Sabbath was made for man, not man for the Sabbath."

~Mark 2:27 (ESV)

In my small designing and remodeling business, I count on reliable service providers who know their area of expertise. When doing the design phase of a remodel project having a solid architect and builder are key to the success of a beautiful, refined finished outcome. Every detail is considered, thought about and incorporated into the plans. If we're doing a kitchen, each drawer, space, cabinet is evaluated, measured and given a purpose. We would never plan a kitchen and forget to plan on where each appliance will be set. All the needs are considered. We give thought to having enough electrical capacity, power, and resources.

God is the designer of the universe and everything in it. He created us. He built us. He considered every nuance of our needs, capacity and potential.

Nothing overlooked or forgotten.

When God designed us, He made us to have limited energy. He created us to need rest. God designed rest. He Himself rested. There was no rest before God thought of it. God created rest before he made us to even need it. It's intentional. Considered. Designed and built in. Ironically, the Pharisees never rested from trying to find Jesus in violation of the Father. Their relentless pursuit of finding blame with Jesus had to have been exhausting!

Once again, Jesus reminds them that rest was God's plan and design, even for them.

Maker of all things, thank you that we fatigue. Thank you that I have limited energy and you planned for my down time. Thank you for restorative love. You are the best rest.

Amen.

How often do you find yourself expending energy in the wrong direction? What can you do to guard your quiet time and rest, so you can be positive and uplifting? God gave you time to rest - how do you use that time?

___

 Rest Fit Tip:

A lack of sleep prevents the body from strengthening the immune system and producing more cytokines to fight infection. This can mean a longer recovery time from illness as well as increased risk of chronic illness.

He Makes A Way

Rebecca Grambort

> "It shall come to pass that before they call, I will answer; and while they are still speaking, I will hear."
>
> ~Isaiah 65:24 (NKJV)

Can you remember a time when God answered you before you called? Early in my faith walk, this would be difficult for me to understand.

It wouldn't be until many moons later that I would receive life-altering "ah-ha" moments that would have me declaring – *'Wow! That was God!'*

That's when I realized that, before I even knew that God was present in my life, He was there, lending me a hand. Have you been in those shoes? Did you ever think that you were working out the details of your life all alone, only to discover that you weren't really alone at all?

It happens one day - you get sucker-punched. You get the news that you have cancer or you lose a loved one to death. You have just set your feet on the road marked with suffering. Then—one day on that road—something crazy happens and you notice that God had pre-arranged a series of events in your life, or strategically placed someone, way in your past, to help you travel that dark and painful road on which you currently find yourself. As you stand there in awe, a wave of peace suddenly floods your entire being.

It all makes sense in reverse and you realize that He answered even before you called.

Did you know that Jesus was the first Person strategically placed in your life? He was! God answered and made a way for you even before the fall of mankind in the garden. Well before sin entered the world, He anticipated the need for salvation and implemented a plan for the redemption of His people through the shed blood of Jesus Christ.

If God did not withhold His precious Son from us, how much more can we trust Him to prearrange a solution for our every problem or need that comes our way? Will you trust your unknown future to an all-knowing God?

Father God, thank You that You answer me before I call!

Amen.

Rest. Reflect. Recall and journal some moments when God prearranged something or someone in advance to help you in your hour of need. Reflect on how the plan of salvation was in place to save you before you were even born. Does His promise to answer before you call give you confidence that you can now rest—even about your current difficulties? Tell God how it feels to serve a God who answers before you even call.

_____

 Rest Fit Tip:

Rough day? Cast your cares on the Lord in prayer or take a few minutes to journal your thoughts before your head hits the pillow.

GOD FORGIVES AND FORGETS

Danelle Skinner

> "If we confess our sins, He is faithful and just and will forgive us our sins and purify us from all unrighteousness."
>
> ~1 John 1:9 (NIV)

Guilt, shame, and self-condemnation of sin are familiar feelings to our world. They can be paralyzing, hindering our intimacy with God, and making it impossible to truly rest our souls. We often have high views of Christ. We know he is loving, caring, and nurturing. We know he forgives, forgets, and does not condemn, but oftentimes we do not accept the same truth for ourselves. We think; if we were more flawless or if we had not done "this or that" . . . then . . . He could forgive us.

The weight of our sin does not matter the Lord, because it doesn't matter what we have done. It only matters what Jesus has done for us on the cross. When we admit our sins *(from Proverbs 20:27 GNT and 1 John 1:8 NIV)*, accept responsibility for them *(from Psalms 51:3 GNT and James 5:16 TLB)*, and ask Him for forgiveness *(from 1 John 1:9 NIV and Romans 3:23-24 TLB)*. He gives us that undeserved gift. The Lord says this: "....*return to my presence, repent and ask me to help you forgive yourself. I accept you back without condemnation. Jesus died on your behalf. When you repent your sins to me, I no longer see your flaws, sins or imperfection. Their sins and lawless acts I will remember no more.*" (Hebrews 10:17 NIV)

I am so grateful our righteous God does not stop at forgiveness. He forgets our sins completely and wants us to do the same. He doesn't want us paralyzed by living in the past, unable to forgive ourselves. He wants us to move forward. He gives us a lifeline by forgiving, forgetting, and purifying ALL our unrighteousness.

How blessed are we? Let's accept His faithfulness, righteousness, and forgiveness. Grab hold of the lifeline, forgive yourselves, and rest in His grace, love, and forgiveness.

God forgives. Let us repent and rest in His forgiveness.

Dear God, thank You for Your grace, love, and forgiveness. Thank You for purifying me from all my unrighteousness. Please help me to accept Your forgiveness and give me the strength to forgive myself. When guilt, shame, and self-condemnation of my sins surface, help me recognize they are of the enemy and not of You, Lord.

Amen.

Rest Of God

God wants us to never forget what it cost Jesus to pay for our sins, but He forgives instantly, completely, repeatedly, and freely. Have you confessed your sins to the Lord with true repentance? Are there things He has forgiven you for that you are still holding on to? Use the space below to make a list of those things and thank the Lord for His undeserved forgiveness. Then rest knowing you are forgiven.

_____

_____

_____

_____

_____

_____

_____

_____

_____

_____

_____

_____

_____

_____

_____

_____

_____

_____

_____

 Rest Fit Tip:

Visualize yourself in a very calm and relaxing place and position to fall asleep faster.

IN THE DECLARATION OF THE LORD

Rebecca Grambort

"For I know the plans I have for you," declares the Lord, "plans to prosper you and not to harm you, plans to give you a hope and a future."

~Jeremiah 29:11 (NIV)

Declaration (noun) – a passionate and legal binding proclamation; notification; an announcement or broadcast.

Do you find it hard to believe the declaration in Jeremiah? I know that it can be difficult to comprehend at times in the midst of so much heartbreak and suffering. It can seem impossible to understand that God is not harming us when we may, in fact, feel . . . harmed!

But God doesn't just say it - He declares it!

The only way to overcome this stinkin' thinkin' is to rest into the trust of His promise. We must resolve to allow this declaration to rule in our minds, instead of allowing our feelings and our own agendas to reign over us.

I personally would learn this lesson the hard way after the tragic death of my spouse. My own attempts at plotting out my future would only prove to add to my grief which would later bring me to my breaking point; thankfully I might add. Heaven knows, what I was doing wasn't working! If there was going to be any hope for a better future, I would need to bow my will to His, and trust Him at His Word. This decision would become the anchor in my storm. It was in that season where God would perform a miraculous work inside of me, carving away at my own plans while replacing them with His.

Sometimes the only way we can discover what God's plans are for our lives is when our own plans come crumbling down. Even though the process hurt, it did not harm me and I came out unscathed. He made a new future for me and I began to prosper, carrying out His ultimate plans that were for the ultimate good!

Jesus, help me to trust that I am safe in Your care. I believe You when You declare that Your plans are to prosper me and to give me a hope and a future!

Amen.

God's plans for us hold an eternal weight that cannot be crushed or destroyed in the midst of any heartbreak or suffering we will face in this temporal life. In what ways can you allow this declaration to bring you rest and be the anchor in your storm? What would your future look like if you let go of your own agendas and bowed your will to His?

 **Rest Fit Tip:**

Do something to wind down before going to bed such as reading.

BE STILL AND KNOW

Teresa Kliner

"Be still, and know that I am God; I will be exalted among the nations, I will be exalted among the earth."

~Psalm 46:10 (NIV)

We live in a fast-paced busy world. Go, go, go all the time. My common response to people when they ask, *'How are you?'* is *'Busy, but that's life, right?'*

We aren't still very often. When we are, we usually have something else going on to fill our minds and thoughts like television or our to do list for the next day. Why is slowing down and inactivity so tough for us? Maybe because we often equate business with worthiness. Therefore, if we are busy, we are worthy. Most of us would argue and say we would love a day to just do nothing. However, when we have those moments, we struggle to be still and know.

What does that even mean? Be still and know?

Webster's definition of "know" is: to be aware of the truth: be convinced or certain of

How often do we stop and have awareness that God is God and will be exalted among the nations? Certain that He is who He says He is. Convinced that He will fulfill His promises for us. Aware of the truth that He loves us and is our protector.

I am guilty of trying to do it all on my own. Hustling for my worth. Working to look good on the outside, while I am crumbling on the inside. Today I am learning to let go, sit still in His presence, and be convinced that He will be exalted for being who He says He is.

Lord, forgive me for trying to go at it on my own. For attempting to be god in my life. You are who You say You are. You are mighty. You are powerful. You are faithful. Right now, I choose to still myself in Your presence and soak in Your faithfulness in my life. I choose to praise You. Help me to walk through this day in Your peace.

Amen.

Close your eyes and take a deep breathe. Sit in God's presence for a moment and just feel His mighty power. Do you struggle with hustling for your worth? What hinders you from being still? What is something that would help you to be still? How can you implement that into your daily life?

 Rest Fit Tip:

Yawning, moodiness, fatigue, irritability, depressed mood, difficulty learning new concepts, forgetfulness, inability to concentrate, lack of motivation, clumsiness, increased appetite, and carbohydrate cravings all indicate a lack of sleep.

HE IS EVERYWHERE

Kathy Carter

"May his left hand be under my head, and his right arm embrace me."
~Song of Songs 2:6 (CSB)

When I was in a Bible Study, I was asked to close my eyes and picture the face of God. What I pictured then, and what I picture today has truly evolved over the years, without me even realizing it, until recently.

God used to seem so far away, out of reach, high on a cross or up in heaven, only to be reunited with when I passed from this earth and my soul went to heaven. I felt He was always looking down on me, but never present in the room next to me. When I closed my eyes, I could see only a sad face or sometimes no face at all.

Growing up, my church had a cross at the front of the church and Jesus on that cross didn't feel warm or inviting. Religion was always ritual for me. Memorized prayers, church on Sundays, typical childhood sin, rinse and repeat. I believed there was a God but I had no relationship with Him. In fact, I did not even own a bible. If I had, I may have stumbled upon Song of Songs 2:6.

In the Song of Songs, God is showing His love and grace all at once. The left hand of Jesus Christ supports us with joy and His right arm shows intense peace and security. Today, God is present in the room, holding my hand, even wrapping His arms around me. He is my friend, my Father, my husband, my everything. When I close my eyes now, I see a warm face, a tender smile, welcoming and caring eyes, and an invitation to sit and be in His presence. A bond so tight that no one can break it. Today I know I can rest in God's arms and He will be with me to eternity.

Dear God, Thank You for being in our presence at all times – sharing our joy, catching us when we fall and carrying us when we are too exhausted to continue. I am sorry that I sometimes forget You are here and I try to conform to the ways of the world. It is my hope to listen to Your voice at all times and reach out to You for guidance in all things. In Your name, Jesus Christ.

Amen.

Rest Of God

Close your eyes and envision Jesus Christ. Write down what you see. What does His face and eyes look like? Is He close to you? Holding you? Or far off? When you picture His arms embracing you, like in Song of Songs 2:6, are you able to feel the rest His Presence brings?

Rest Fit Tip:

Evaluate your mattress and pillow and make sure they are comfortable yet supportive.

FAITH BRINGS REST

Margaret Bentham-Moe

> "And He said, My presence shall go with thee, and I will give thee rest. And he said unto Him, if Thy presence go not with me, carry us not hence."
>
> ~Exodus 33:14-15 (KJV)

The Christmas season is the one time of year that the whole family is together. When my daughter was a flight attendant, there was one year when she had to be away on Christmas Day. It was the first time that we weren't all together for Christmas breakfast. It wasn't the same, looking around the table and not seeing ALL of the children there. Have you ever looked forward to an event because your best friend would be going along but your friend had to cancel? That could diminish your enjoyment. What if Your friend was God and He had decided He would no longer go with you?

I can't imagine how Moses felt when God said He wouldn't accompany the Israelites into the Promised Land. As far as Moses was concerned, possessing the land without the presence of God was meaningless and he might as well remain where he was. The people's behavior was the reason for God's decision. They made a golden calf with the jewelry they had taken from the Egyptians when they left Egypt, worshipped the image, and did abominable things. They did so because Moses went up to the mountain to return in forty days. During that time, there was no sign of him. They surmised that he had died and failed to consider what God had already done for them. Because they lacked faith, they had no rest.

Moses' petition on behalf of Israel resulted in God, not only agreeing to go with them, but His promise of giving them rest as well. Therein lies the lesson for us: our rest is in God and we can only have rest when we desire His presence more than anything else. The Israelites were about to enter the Promised Land, but they would also have to drive out the current inhabitants. That does not sound like an occasion for rest, so it must mean that the *Rest of God* is not the absence of activity, challenges, or trials, but faith in God to give us the victory. Faith in God is the precursor for being in His rest and *Hebrews 4:13* tells us so. *"For unto us was the gospel preached as well as unto them; but the word preached did not profit them, not being mixed with faith in them that heard it. For we which have believed do enter into His rest."*

If we lack faith in God we will not be able to rest in God either.

Father, when we fail to have faith in You we also forfeit Your rest. Please forgive us and by Your Grace help us to rest in You. In Jesus Name.

Amen.

Isn't it wonderful that we can have both God's presence and His rest? In what area of your life are you not enjoying God's rest right now? Since faith and rest are directly linked, evaluate your faith in this area. In ways are you believing God and in what ways aren't you believing God? Write a prayer of gratitude to God for His presence and in supplication for His rest.

_____
_____
_____
_____
_____
_____
_____
_____
_____
_____
_____
_____
_____
_____
_____
_____
_____
_____
_____

 Rest Fit Tip:

Some consider sleep as wasted time and purposely deprive themselves of sleep to pursue other things such as entertainment, educational goals, or money-making pursuits. This intentional sleep deprivation is most likely to be seen in teenagers and young adults.

GET AWAY WITH ME

Candice Moe

"Are you tired? Worn out? Burned out on religion? Come to Me. Get away with Me and you'll recover your Life. I'll show you how to take a real rest. Walk with Me and work with Me—watch how I do it. Learn the unforced rhythms of Grace. I won't lay anything heavy or ill-fitting on you. Keep company with Me and you'll learn to Live freely and lightly."

~Matthew 11:28-30 MSG

Grace is commonly spoken of but did you know Grace is a person? Love is a person, as is victory. Christ is the embodiment of these, they exude from His very Being. Are you exhausted by the rigors of life and the rudiments of religion? "Come!" An invitation from the Lover of your soul ... "Come!"

Begrudgingly, I heard of everything that needed discarding, of all I couldn't do as a Christian. In reading the Bible, I realized emphasis should be, in fact, on all that I could do! I remember struggling with sin and I also remember the day my struggles were quelled. It was the day I chose Grace, the second I chose to rest in the finished work of Jesus Christ. Grace is not an excuse to sin but an empowerment to live void of it! In 2011, I surrendered myself to Jesus and quickly discovered—the closer I drew towards Him—the less I hankered after sin. *James 1:14 MSG* says, *"Temptation comes from our own desires, which entice us and drag us away."* When I first read that verse, I sussed the key to living sin free was inheriting Godly desires. Abba's fancies had to become my inclinations.

As I reminisce, what's staggering is how effortlessly sinful predispositions I once struggled with have lost their appeal. While my Bible consumption mushroomed, my disdain for sin burgeoned. Spending quality time reading the Bible enkindles a metamorphosis of heart. You see, on the cross, Jesus did the work for us. Our response ought to be one of receiving, not of striving. A new heart is a tall order, one only the Holy Spirit can facilitate.

Am I avowing that daily perusal alone is sufficient? No. We must read, but we must also choose to come into agreement with the Word of God. *James 1:22 MSG* explains, *"But don't just listen to God's Word. You must do what it says. Otherwise, you are only fooling yourselves."* Synchronization of study and application is imperative. Resting in the completeness of Calvary's Cross is a symphony of twain.

Father help me to cease from toiling and realize clean hearts come only from You. I ask for passionate comprehension of Your Word with quality time to read it. I rest in Your enabling Grace to implement Your teachings, in Jesus' Name.

Amen.

In what ways have you grappled to change yourself? What things do you think you still need to discard in your life? How can you rest in Abba's Grace and ask Him to help you on your journey to be clean? Allow God space and time later today to calm you and gift you with His rest. Describe what that will look like.

Rest Fit Tip:

Avoid too many liquids or caffeine too close to bedtime so your sleep isn't interrupted by trips to the bathroom.

God's Assurance

Jane Guffy

> "But as he considered these things, behold, an angel of the Lord appeared to him in a dream, saying, "Joseph, son of David, do not fear to take Mary as your wife, for that which is conceived in her is from the Holy Spirit."
> ~Matthew 1:20 (ESV)

God recognizes things about us that we don't. Joseph was simply "considering" these things, but the angel calls it fear. God comforted Joseph's fear about ALL these things.

Our oldest son made us Papa and Gigi. I can relate to Joseph as he "considered these things" as the news of our pregnancy was unexpected and out of sequence, like Mary. I wish an angel had appeared to me in a dream to explain! That would have been really helpful! Instead, God wanted us to meet Him, with dependence, need, faith, tears, fear and a thousand other emotions.

Joseph was given the gift of rest through divine assurance. I needed that!

God's assurance landed on me when He revealed to our son and his (now) wife, that they would be parents to identical twin, yummy girls. I saw this as a sign that God was present and carrying the weight, so we could be calm. He had this all figured out and I could rest in His plan. You see our brown-eyed son is a fraternal twin, so he could claim no boast in the DNA of these beautiful, blue-eyed girls, since they are identical. The hand of God claimed their fingerprints. It was His intention to have this pregnancy, the unknowns, and anxiety resting in the Word of God "to not fear take her as your wife" and that this conception didn't get past the maker and caregiver of the universe. I needed to rest there and gave Him the rest of it. The rest of our story is a miracle as we now have four grandchildren through our son. The rest of Joseph's story is a miracle for all of us as we became God's children!

God uses our rest time to meet us. Joseph was dreaming, sleeping. We need relief, a time to reflect and be quiet. God created our need to stop and pause. Let's give God opportunities to meet us by being still.

Heavenly Father, Your infinite mercy, grace, and love are the perfect resting place. Thank You.

Amen.

What is a situation you need God's assurance in right now? Ask Him for it in your journaling today. Allow God space and time later today to calm you and gift you with His rest. Describe what that will look like.

 Rest Fit Tip:

Cold feet? Slip on some socks! Having warm hands and feet can help you fall asleep faster.

Rest In The Right Path

Marlene Dawson

"It shall come to pass that before they call, I will answer; and while they are still speaking, I will hear."

~Isaiah 57:2 (NASB)

My brother Terry came home to visit after being honorably discharged from the Air Force. He and our younger brothers decided to camp overnight in the mountains. It was the first time they made such a trek, and they were, shall I say, unprepared? Mom called the rescue team when they were several hours late.

The Captain wanted to know who was left handed, explaining, "People who are left handed tend to go right when lost, and right-handed people go left, and the oldest decides direction."

Terry is left handed, and I informed the Captain my oldest brother would be giving the orders.

He studied his maps, pointed to an access road, and said, "They will probably come back on this road."

Two members of the team started running up the access road, and within ten minutes we heard shouting. "Here they come! They all appear to be okay!"

Mom's eyes watered as her face softened into a restful expression.

There are many paths to follow in life and taking the wrong direction can get us lost. In the Old Testament, those who believed and followed God did not enter God's rest until they died. Isiah 57:2 speaks of a time when God called people to heaven because of a dangerous situation on the horizon. This is a foreshadowing of our New Testament opportunity to pursue Jesus and enter into His rest now.

We can enter the *Rest of God* by choosing to follow Jesus. We begin to follow Jesus when we accept that we are sinners in need of this Savior. We then repent of our sin and ask Jesus to be our Savior and Lord. Then we thank Him and begin to read the Bible. We also look for a Bible believing church where we can learn and grow in this new relationship with the Creator of the universe.

Lord, help me to stay in the place of rest You have provided. I am a woman of integrity because You made me Your daughter. I place my cares in your capable hands. Thank You for taking them and for keeping me.

Amen.

Rest Of God

Life can be very difficult sometimes, but we are assured we have entered God's rest because we choose to follow His ways. Think of a time when you stepped off of God's path. What happened to your peace? What steps did you take to get back to His place of rest?

_____
_____
_____
_____
_____
_____
_____
_____
_____
_____
_____
_____
_____
_____
_____
_____
_____
_____
_____

Rest Fit Tip:

Stick to a sleep schedule of the same bedtime and wake up time, even on the weekends.

Go Back And Try Again!

Tamara Fink

> "In vain you rise early and stay up late, toiling for food to eat—for he grants sleep to those he loves."
>
> ~Psalms 127:2 (NIV)

Have you ever experienced the sheer exhaustion of loss? A friend who has betrayed your confidence? A home lost to bankruptcy? An unfaithful spouse? The death of a child? You're at the end of your proverbial rope and you can't hold on for lack of strength. Yeah, me too.

I've had many people tell me to rest in God's promises, but how can we rest when what we had been working towards didn't come to pass? In this passage of scripture, the writer is calling us out. He's saying our efforts are in vain or, in other words; useless, excessive, and prideful. Woah, that's a tad harsh wouldn't you say? Not really. Read further. He's not referring to us working an honest day's work or doing all we can in a situation. He's talking about us taking on the responsibility of the outcome. He's talking about us not trusting God's love. Instead of worrying and toiling, God is calling us to rest.

When we fully trust God, our sleep is truly restful. As we enter into restful sleep our minds and bodies are refreshed. During this refreshing we are restored and strengthened for the next day. Many times, we have no control over the circumstances that happen to us, but we do have control over how we respond to those circumstances.

I remember, as a little girl, my mom saying, *'Tamara, you choose your attitude and you chose poorly. Go back and try again!'*

My family loves to harass me about mom's advice and, on occasion, one of them will even repeat these words to me or others around us. It's a great reminder for each of us today.

God, today I choose thankfulness. Thankfulness for a mighty God who loves me and wants to offer me rest. I gladly receive Your rest today and I pray that you help me see what I can do and surrender the rest to You. I ask all these things in Jesus name.

Amen.

What will you choose for your focus today? Will it be an attitude of resting in God's promises or will it be an attitude of vain toiling? Ask yourself, "Will I choose to trust God and partake in His rest?" I pray your answer is yes!

Rest Fit Tip:

If you are struggling to fall asleep and it is making you anxious, get up and do something that tires you out and then go back to bed and try again.

HEALED BY THE HAND OF GOD

Marlene Dawson

> "In You, Lord, do I put my trust and seek refuge; let me never be put to shame or [have my hope in You] disappointed; deliver me in Your righteousness."
>
> ~Psalms 31:1 (AMPC)

"The tests were positive. You'll need to go home and plan your baby's funeral." Our pediatrician's voice cracked as he patted my arm.

Jim and I were young believers, but we had recently heard teaching about God's healing power. We asked our home church leaders to pray with us at the hospital. When they finished praying, they handed Betsi to me.

I knew God was the answer to all my prayers, and with tears, I prayed, "Lord, we would sure like to have Betsi with us for a while longer, but if she needs to be with you more than she needs to be with us, then please take her home soon. Amen."

God's Presence filled the room, bringing rest and peace. It would be several years before I learned this is what entering God's rest looks like. As Betsi's vitals improved immediately, tests were re-ordered forty-eight hours later. This time, all of her tests came back negative, and the doctor wrote "Healed by the hand of God" on her chart.

God is always faithful and trustworthy. Sometimes our minds and bodies just go to that fearful or stress filled place. This is when we need to remind ourselves of God's complete faithfulness. *Proverbs 12:21 (AMPC)* tells us *"No [actual] calamity shall come upon the righteous...."* This means it may look and feel like a calamity, but it is not.

We do not need to become stressed as we go through earthly trials. Oh, sure, we will still have trials and tribulations, but we can trust in knowing God will never allow us to be ashamed for putting our trust in the living God. He is our refuge, our place of rest. We can rely on God's understanding and compassion. He knows we are but flesh and bone. God is not thrown off by our imperfections; He desires to become our strength in the midst of them.

Father God, there are times I have been afraid to trust You. Help me in my unbelief. Thank you, Lord.

Amen.

Rest Of God

We can rely on God's understanding and compassion. Think of a time when you didn't trust God would see you through a difficult situation. How did His Word sustain you? When did you remember He is always faithful, no matter how difficult life gets?

_____
_____
_____
_____
_____
_____
_____
_____
_____
_____
_____
_____
_____
_____
_____
_____
_____
_____
_____
_____
_____

 Rest Fit Tip:

Feeling revved up at bedtime? Deep breathing stimulates the body's calming system. Try a few rounds of inhaling and exhaling slowly.

So, You Truly Think You're Going To Rest Today?

Luanne Nelson

> "So they went away by themselves in a boat to a solitary place."
> ~Mark 6:32 (NIV)

Taking a personal time out to regroup by resting in the midst of personal and professional noise is holy. Jesus did it and showed his disciples how to do it. On the day of this verse, the disciples wanted to escape the crowd, hurrying offshore for some peace and quiet. Certainly, it was a relief to flee from the noise the multitude of people were making on the shoreline. Little did those disciples know that the same crowd would be running to the other side of the shoreline to greet them upon their arrival, hungry for both food and more of what Jesus had to say about life. Jesus knew. He knew they were all sheep without a shepherd. Jesus knew he was about to deliver a huge lesson about mercy and being of service. His disciples were clueless. Are you open to spiritual epiphanies?

Jesus not only taught his disciples how to preach, He had also given them ability to perform miracles. They thought they were escaping together to rest and to ask Jesus questions over a quiet dinner on the other side of the lake. Little did they know five thousand people would be showing up for dinner with them. Loaves and fishes for everyone! When life happens, we have to be prepared to help people no matter how sleepy we are. Only through our Savior can we truly have the right attitude of gratitude when called to serve. With Jesus, we can be confident everything will fall into place perfectly.

We do not know God's plans. I'm certain the disciples had quite the adrenalin rush sharing dinner with 5,000 people, seeing the miracle of the loaves and fishes and hearing Jesus deliver His famous Sermon on the Mount that day. I'm sure they slept well that night.

Lord God Almighty, please teach me how to hear Your voice and Your voice only when the noise of life gets too loud. Teach me how to completely trust You!

Amen.

Have you been asked by the Father to open your heart for someone in need when you were exhausted? You may have been tired physically, but did you experience a spiritual rest? Jesus said, *"Blessed are the merciful, for they will be shown mercy." (Matthew 5:7 NIV)* How did God show you mercy for your act of mercy?

_____
_____
_____
_____
_____
_____
_____
_____
_____
_____
_____
_____
_____
_____
_____
_____
_____
_____
_____
_____
_____
_____

Rest Fit Tip:

Sleep deprivation causes the release of insulin, which leads to increased fat storage and a higher risk of Type 2 Diabetes.

Give God The Right To Direct your Life

Kimberly Joy Krueger

> "Give God the right to direct your life, and as you trust him along the way you'll find He pulled it off perfectly."
>
> ~Psalms 37:5 (TPT)

"The Holy Spirit is a gentleman." I heard my mom say it time and time again.

As a young child, I could only picture a man opening a door for a lady. That is who a gentleman was in my book. I wondered why in the world my mom would compare the Holy Spirit to a man opening a door? Isn't it funny what kids come up with? Even as a "kid" in the faith, I still did not know what she meant. After getting to know God, through His Word, I finally understood. A gentleman does not "force" himself upon you. A gentleman lets you have your preference. A gentleman offers his help and graciously accepts your denial when you refuse him. The Holy Spirit is definitely a gentleman. There are times I wish He weren't. Once in a while, when I'm telling God how amazing He is and what a brilliant job He did on creation, I gently chide Him with 'except for that whole free-will part.' I know my life would be a lot easier if I didn't have so many choices! (And I seem to have a propensity for choosing the bad ones!) What if God just decided for me? Or what if I was just hardwired to obey Him? Life would be so much easier if He just controlled my choices!

Throughout my life, I've encountered a few too many people that wanted to control me and my choices and I must admit, I have a bit of an aversion to it. (Okay, I have a big aversion to it!) I'm so grateful God is not demanding His right to control me! No, He is, in fact, a gentleman, as my mother so aptly stated. He does not force Himself upon us. He does not make us do things His way. He doesn't even punish us when we don't! He kindly and graciously stands in wait at a door for us that leads to inner peace and rest, knowing we may not choose to walk through it. And He is not angry or offended when we don't. That is some serious class right there. We do have the right to direct our own lives. He gave that right to us. That is precisely what free will is. To experience a deep abiding rest, though, to see God's plan for our lives pulled off perfectly, we must relinquish that right back to Him. We must say not only once, but again and again, "God, I give you the right to direct my life because I trust you! I will keep trusting you along the way because I know You are the only one who can pull it off perfectly!"

God, I give You the right to direct my life because I trust You! I will keep trusting You along the way because I know You are the only one who can pull it off perfectly!

Amen.

Are you willing to give God the right to direct your life today? Which areas of your life will you turn over to Him? Which are the hardest to turn over to Him? Why? Will you consider offering your prayer of relinquishment in writing today?

 **Rest Fit Tip:**

Daily exercise leads to better, deeper sleep.

People In Training

Lisa Danegelis

> "I waited patiently for the Lord; and He inclined to me, and heard my cry. He also brought me up out of a horrible pit, out of the miry clay, and set my feet upon a rock, and established my steps."
>
> ~Psalms 40:1-2 (NKJV)

My pit has been deep and isolating for years. It is unusual and particularly evil, crafted by the ravages of psychiatric drugs. In trying to care for insomnia that caused struggles in my mental health, I was incorrectly prescribed drugs that unfortunately caused even more issues. The prescribed drugs had psychoactive effects that I didn't expect. However, going off the drugs was even more damaging to my body.

At times, my condition is scoffed at by others and easily misunderstood. Onlookers have walked by my pit and peered in with an array of responses. A few have thrown in their litter without a glance. Others have given a quick wave and forced smile as they hurry on, and some have hesitantly reached in. But a rare few have climbed in, held my hand, kissed my tear stained face, and loved me in my brokenness.

There are riches in the dark.

I love this acronym for the pit: (P) people (I) in (T) training. Joseph's pit, which was fraught with betrayal, slavery, and imprisonment led to him to the palace. Paul's pit of beatings, starvation, and shipwreck led to the rapid spread of the Gospel. Moses' pit of exile and wilderness wanderings led to freedom for the Israelites.

Are you in a pit? Maybe you crawled down there yourself due to poor choices, or maybe God hand selected your pit and dropped you in. If you're like me, you have probably asked...no...begged Him to rescue you. Maybe you have kicked and screamed, trying to claw your way out, only to sink back down in despair. And maybe (like me), you tried to work your way out by praising, praying, repenting, fasting, and even bargaining!

Well friends, if there is one thing this pit-dweller has learned, it is this: Pits designed by God have only one key and God holds it close to His heart. So settle in and embrace His plan. His timing is perfect and your destiny may very well be awaiting when He pulls you out.

Heavenly Father, shine Your light into my pit and help me see the hidden treasures as I wait on You.

Amen.

Are you in a pit? Is it of your own making or has God thrown you in? Journal about your pit and how you arrived. Ask God to show you what you are to learn, and if there is anything you could do to shorten the time. Be honest about your fears and frustrations and put them in the Father's hands. And finally, envision what your life may look like when those doors fling open!

 Rest Fit Tip:

Sleep deprivation can kill your sex drive, age your skin, and make you forgetful. Make getting a minimum of seven to nine hours of sleep a priority.

Let God Fight Your Battles

Susan Brozek

"The LORD will fight for you; you need only to be still."

~Exodus 14:14 (NIV)

I've always been the type of person who is strongly driven and adopts the mentality: *'if I want something to get done, I need to be self-sufficient and independent, and rely on my own resources.'*

While I believe there may be a place for this attitude, there is much more to be said for coming to the end of ourselves and our own self-effort and fully surrendering to God, while leaning entirely on His sufficiency! He knows what we need in order to accomplish what He has asked us to do and, if He has brought us to it, He will most certainly bring us through it. This is especially true when matters are out of our control, and we are forced to rely entirely on His provision and supply.

If we look around at our circumstances, instead of looking up to God, we risk discouragement. God wants us to realize that He can deliver us from any situation, even if—on the surface—it appears impossible . . . because He is the God of the Impossible!

When we place ourselves and our circumstances entirely in His hands, we are proving that we trust Him as our *El Shaddai*, the God of all Sufficiency. How much moreso then should we "be still" and rest, knowing that God is at work on our difficulty? We can cease from striving while He arranges circumstances, brings forth His favor and provision, and orchestrates answers to our dilemmas as we wait upon Him. If He can part the Red Sea for the Israelites, imagine what He can do for us when we truly let Him fight our battles!

Dear Heavenly Father, I ask that You teach me what it means to be still and to rest in You. Help me to let go of everything that I hold onto so tightly, release my concerns and circumstances into Your capable hands, and allow You to fight for me.

Amen.

In what areas of your life do you feel that you need to take your hands off a given situation so that God can put His hands on it? What would need to happen for you to fully let go of some areas of your life where you have been striving and fighting your own battles? How would your life be different on a day-to-day basis if you truly learned to rest in His supply?

 **Rest Fit Tip:**

Eliminate loud noise and light from your bedroom for uninterrupted sleep.

DISCOVERING DAY SEVEN

Kimberly Joy Krueger

"For only we who believe can enter his rest. As for the others, God said, "In my anger I took an oath: 'They will never enter my place of rest,'" even though this rest has been ready since he made the world."

~Hebrews 4:3 (NLT)

From the first week of creation, there was a provision made for rest. Have you ever wondered why? I mean, He's God, so He didn't do it because He was tired. There is a priceless lesson—that I almost didn't learn—hidden in the simple words, "so on the seventh day he rested from all His work." Creation week was a lot like my walk with the Lord over the last twenty-six years. From the first day, I went to work! Day 1 – I said, "let there be light" as I attempted to fix and change the people I loved; but I secretly worried they never would. Day 2 – I brought forth water to clean up our "Jerry Springer Show"; but I worried that we'd need the security detail to jump up on the stage and 'break it up' anyway. Day 3 – I scoured the land for enough "vegetation" to feed my small army three square meals a day; but I worried that there wouldn't be enough to go around. Day 4 – Who needs God's sun, moon, and stars? I did my best to be all three to my husband and children; but I worried that I'd never measure up. Day 5 – I homeschooled my children, taking them on ample field trips to witness the wonders of sky and sea; but I worried about the day my flock would fly away. Day 6 – I even did my part to "be fruitful and multiply" as I filled the earth with children (that seemed—at times—like animals); but I worried that I'd never be the patient mother they needed. I had it all figured out—just ask me! I worked hard to be Father, Son, and Holy Spirit in my life and the lives of my loved ones. And I seriously had no idea why it wasn't working! After years of work and worry, I got a clue. Day 7 – I discovered rest.

I finally saw that only God has the power to change the things I was trying to change and that His grace covered us all while we learned. I began to trust God with our needs and our brokenness. For the first time, I experienced what the Strong's Concordance calls rest: "a fixed and tranquil place; a calming of the winds." And oh . . . did these winds need calming! When I stopped trusting in me and started trusting in Him, He said, "Peace. Be still," to my storm. I finally discovered Day 7; but it took a while! If I were to compare my walk with the Lord to creation week, I would definitely say I worked six days and rested one. I was late to that party, but I did arrive! How about you?

Are you ready to cease striving and to rest in God's Grace and Promises? Heaven's provision is flowing to every area of our lives right now—and it never stops. But when we spend all of our days in work and worry, we delay our discovery of Day 7. We choke out the Heavenly supply line and cut ourselves off from the incredible abundance of rest available to us when we trust in Him.

Lord, I confess that I have worried, worked, and strived to fix and change things in myself and the ones I love. I have attempted to provide and protect; but that is Your job. Today, I choose to rest in Your unlimited power, provision, promises, and peace.

Amen.

Are you able to rest in God's grace and promises in the middle of your "Creation Week?" Can you apply His grace to yourself, or are you still working and worrying through your days? What about the ones you love? Are you able to release them to His care and allow Him to calm the winds?

_____
_____
_____
_____
_____
_____
_____
_____
_____
_____
_____
_____
_____
_____
_____
_____
_____
_____
_____
_____

Rest Fit Tip:

Getting the right amount of sleep is crucial to your health. Sleep helps with motivation and mood. When you don't get enough sleep it's easier to cancel your workouts and accidentally overeat in an attempt to gain more energy.

Rest, Don't Fret

Susan Brozek

"Rest in the LORD, and wait patiently for Him; do not fret because of him who prospers in his way, because of the man who brings wicked schemes to pass."
~Psalm 37:7 (NKJV)

There have been times in my life when I have felt stuck because I did not seem to be making a difference for God. Meanwhile, others prosper, while not giving His Kingdom a second thought. God's Word instructs us as to how we should respond to such situations. He knows that in my flesh, I might want to cry out, *'Why, God? This hardly seems fair!'* And He certainly doesn't condemn me when I do react like that, but He in His infinite wisdom encourages us to rest and wait instead. This is no easy task, because emotions are involved, along with our fleshly tendency to lack perspective.

He exhorts us to not fret. Most of us view fretting as some form of worrying. Interestingly, it is much more than that. Fretting comes from the Hebrew word "charah," meaning 'to be hot, furious, burn, become angry, be kindled or incensed, or to heat oneself in vexation.' The true meaning of "fret" is very intense! It comes from a Hebrew word picture of being "fenced in." So, if we feel we have had a hedge surrounding us while others appear to prosper, we can easily become resentful, extremely frustrated, envious, angry . . . we can heat ourselves in vexation! It is at this very moment that our God asks us to rest. Although this may superficially sound counterintuitive, God always knows the best times to send down blessings upon us because He is Jehovah El Roi, the God who sees, and He sees perfectly when blessings may cause us to become prideful or stumble in some way. He encourages us to wait upon His timing and, when He asks us to wait, it is always and only for our highest good.

Lord God, we know that waiting upon You and being patient takes more inner strength than receiving Your blessings when we believe the time is right in our eyes to receive them. Give us an extra portion of your strength when we find ourselves in situations where we need to rest and not fret.

Amen.

Are there times when you find yourself resentful, envious, or angry in noticing the blessings of others? What is your typical response? Think of a recent situation when you may have felt you deserved something that another person received. Describe what happened in your heart. Did you process through your emotions with the Lord? What might need to happen in the future for you to be content in resting and waiting, versus fretting and burning?

Rest Fit Tip:

Improper sleep can cause weight gain, accidents, and irritability.

ENTER GOD'S REST – HEAVEN ON EARTH

Candice Moe

> "There remaineth therefore a Rest to the people of God. For he that is entered into His Rest, he also hath ceased from his own works, as God did from His. Let us labour therefore to enter into that Rest, lest any man fall after the same example of unbelief."
>
> ~Hebrews 4:9-11 (KJV)

"Labor to enter His rest...." It sounds rather oxymoronic doesn't it? Admittedly, they do appear polar opposites. The labor spoken of by apostle Paul, is when we disrobe self-effort and striving, choosing instead to put on Christ. The world need worry about what to wear, what to eat, what to put on, (Matthew 6) but as a blood-washed believer, you've been adopted into a family where your Daddy is King! As a regal offspring, all things essential and desirous are opulently supplied, simply because of who your patriarch is. Your Patriarch is Abba, Father.

After salvation, we're newborns, engendered to live on earth as it is in Heaven. Instantly our spirits are pristine, but our souls must be renewed by daily reading the Word of God . . . training for flourishing.

How can I improve my social standing? How do I get ahead in life and my career? Should I apply for this job or that promotion? When will I get married . . . who do I marry? Is the tick tock of that good 'ole biological clock deafening to anyone else? What do I do now? Why did that friendship end?

Life presents many questions and worry attempts to disguise itself as beneficial, while striving falsifies as a solution. The Bible assures you that your Father has left no hour or aspect of your life to chance. He is not figuring out His plan for you as you go along. Jesus extends an open invitation for you to talk with Him in prayer about each decision you ought to make. His Spirit wants to lead you into the victorious life your Heavenly Father has already prepared. You were created on purpose with purpose for purpose. *Psalm 139:16 TLB says, "You saw me before I was born and scheduled each day of my life before I began to breathe. Every day was recorded in Your book!"*

Do you truly believe that your Father Loves you and has good plans for you? (Jeremiah 29:11) Rest in His love, willingness, and ability to guide you beside still waters and lead you in the paths of Righteousness and success. (Psalm 84:11).

Father, help me to know Your heart for me. Help me dwell in Your rest, trusting completely in You. Remind me to ask for Your guidance always, in Jesus' Name.

Amen.

What were the results of your most recent decisions? How could you have rested in the outcome even before it came? Do you have questions that still linger for which you need to pray for God to give you Rest in the outcome? Write that prayer, below.

___

 **Rest Fit Tip:**

To avoid snoring, sleep on your side.

THE LORD WAITS FOR YOU; DO YOU WAIT FOR HIM?

Danelle Skinner

"So the LORD must wait for you to come to him so he can show you his love and compassion. For the LORD is a faithful God. Blessed are those who wait for his help."

~Isaiah 30:18 (NIV)

Jesus is always present, patiently waiting for us to turn our attention to Him. He said, *"Whoever drinks the water I give will never thirst." (John 4:14 NIV)*

Imagine a water bottle. It is present but waiting for us to turn our attention to it for a drink. The water purifies, cleans, and flushes out toxins. Jesus is asking us to turn our focus to Him, so that we can recognize, and truly experience the fullness of His blessings. He purifies, cleanses, and flushes out evil from our lives.

As a nation, we have lost the joy of waiting. We are addicted to noise, busyness, and speed. Instant gratification is the norm and most things we want can be achieved as fast as the click of a button. Despite that, can you remember a time you eagerly waited in anticipation for something? With each passing day, did happiness, excitement, and joy build?

Sometimes the Lord's help is instant. Other times, He asks us to wait for His blessings.

Imagine a pregnant woman. As she waits for the blessing of her baby to arrive, she does not just wait. She waits with anticipation of what is to come. She knows there will be a blessing. She does not know when, where, or how. Yet she knows it will come and she prepares. She waits, she rests, and she nourishes her body, so that she will be fully ready for her blessing's arrival.

While we wait on the Lord for our blessings, He is not withholding something from us. He is preparing us by purifying, cleansing, and transforming our hearts. He renews our minds, restores our energy, and empowers us to do what He calls us to do, making sure our body, mind, and soul are fully ready for our blessings when they arrive. When we focus our attention on Him, we can recognize the blessings of His love and compassion, regain balance, face uncertainty with peace, and find joy. Like an expectant mother, let's eagerly wait in anticipation and prepare for our blessings by nourishing our spirits with the Word of God. Happiness, excitement, and joy will build.

Lord, thank You for waiting on me. Thank You for blessing me with Your love, compassion, and faithfulness. Thank You for preparing my body, mind, and soul for Your blessings. I will wait on You!

Amen.

Blessed are the Lord's people. God loves you, He cares for you and He wants to bless you. He is transforming you and maybe He's not done yet! What is the Lord asking you to wait on Him for? Are you willing to wait until He is done preparing you for your blessing?

Rest Fit Tip:

To unwind your mind and emotions, avoid all screen time or bright lights for forty-five minutes before bedtime.

Resting In His Presence

Teresa Kliner

> "Do not be anxious about anything, but in everything, by prayer and petition, with thanksgiving, present your requests to God. And the peace of God, which transcends all understanding will guard your hearts and mind in Christ Jesus."
> ~Philippians 4: 6-7 (NIV)

Anxiety hits us all at different times and levels. For some, it's trying that new exercise move at the gym, presenting your new idea at work, or confronting someone. For others, it peers its ugly head for no apparent reason. When my daughter was younger, she often worried. Bedtime seemed to be the hardest. So we made her a "worry box" and I told her that once she wrote her worry out and put it in the box, she couldn't think about it anymore. This became part of our bedtime routine. For her to get a peaceful night sleep I would have her…

> Brush her teeth
> Write out her worries and stick them in her box
> Pray
> Close her eyes
> Sleep

God's peace is beyond anything we can fathom and it is a protection for our hearts and our minds. However, we have to do a couple things to receive God's peace. Just like my daughter had steps to get a peaceful night's sleep. We, too, have steps we need to do, in order to rest in God's peace.

> First we need understand that we have control over our hijacking thoughts.
> Next we need to stop and pray with thanksgiving and praise.
> Then we rest in God's peace that is beyond our understanding –
> peace when nothing makes sense.

I don't know about you, but I tend to want a short cut. Feel anxious and go straight to the peace that passes all understanding. This isn't the plan. We need to be willing to follow the steps to be able to rest in His incomprehensible peace.

Lord we praise You and thank you for being who You are. We thank You for loving us and caring about each and everything we deal with. Lord we bring to You our day. We lay it and all that comes with it in Your hands. Lord guard our hearts and minds, in You, I pray.

Amen.

We all experience anxiety and nervousness at times. It's how we deal with it that makes a difference. What is something you are anxious or nervous about right now? What steps can you take today to receive God's peace?

 Rest Fit Tip:

Low blue spectrum light helps your brain reset for sleep and increases melatonin (which aids in sleep). Try low blue light exposure for about three hours before bed.

His Eyes

Kathy Carter

"Casting all your cares on Him, because He cares about you."

~1 Peter 5:7 (CSB)

I remember, as a teenager, crying so hard with my dog, feeling so hurt, and thinking he was the only one on the planet that cared. I really felt that he understood my pain even though I couldn't hear him speak. It was in his eyes that I saw comfort. He wouldn't leave my side until he knew I was okay. It was an unconditional love that I had never felt so strongly about. Sadly, he was hit by a car when I was not ready for his passing.

Are we ever ready for a loss that is truly deep in our hearts . . . that deep hole that feels so empty?

The love of a pet is undeniable and so is God's love, but here is the difference, God will never leave our side. He will never give up on us and His love will never run out. Like a pet, it is unconditional. Unlike a pet, He will always be waiting for us when we open the door. We just need to reach out our hands and seek His heart and truths in everything we do. He is excited to fill our hearts with His love and be with us throughout eternity.

1 Peter 5:7 says to *"Cast all our cares and worries on our Lord Jesus."* He cares for us and we will never have to be alone or afraid. His comforting presence is with us always. Whenever you feel hurt, anxious or alone, have faith in the Lord, for He is always waiting for you with open arms.

Dear God, Thank You so much for always being there for us and caring for us in all things. You are amazing, God, and I pray that I will always remember to seek You first, especially in times of worry and unrest. In Your name, Lord Jesus Christ.

Amen.

Think of a time when you have experienced a great loss from a broken friendship, what was your initial reaction to coping with the feeling of emptiness? What would it look like if God were in the room with you as your friend, comforting you and holding your hand?

Rest Fit Tip:

Insufficient sleep can affect female hormone production, growth hormones in children, and testosterone in men.

RETREAT IN SOLITUDE

Tracy Hennes

"Yet the news about him spread all the more, so that crowds of people came to hear him and to be healed of their sicknesses. But Jesus often withdrew to lonely places and prayed."

~ Luke 5:15-16 (NIV)

There are many daily demands on our time and energy. This is especially true in our western-world culture. We are a results-based society, pressured to keep moving, do more, have more, achieve greater. We run around more, work longer, entertain larger, and burn harder. We are overworked, over-scheduled, over-stimulated, and over-stressed. Heart disease and stroke run rampant in our world, yet they are highly preventable. We may be filling our schedules with worthwhile activities, but at what cost to our own health? What good are we to the people we care about if we don't take care of ourselves?

Jesus often withdrew to lonely places . . . left, pulled away, retreated, to be alone. The biblical rock star of all ages was healing people, preaching to them, changing lives, and he knew the value of rest and solitude. No matter what our work is, taking a break is critical for our well-being. Just as Jesus would go on quiet reprieve, we must take time to draw our awareness away from the external world and direct our attention inward and upward.

While a weeklong, lakeside, mountain retreat sounds amazing, few of us can afford such luxury. We can, however, make room in our schedules and environment for our own mini-retreats; take a walk, slow down to sip a latte, unplug from the computer and enjoy the sunshine, go for a scenic drive, claim quiet time for prayer, hang a "do not disturb" sign and take a nap or a bath. When we quiet our minds and bodies, we regather our energy, and experience sounds and thoughts in a new way. We may rediscover creativity, develop greater empathy, remember who we are, and encounter Christ. To be the best version of ourselves, we should practice rest and solitude regularly.

Jesus, help me to be more like You as I care for myself and others. Please help me to experience the richness the Holy Spirit brings to my quiet times.

Amen.

When you allow yourself to merely think of a relaxing retreat, what do you notice happens to your breathing? Does it slow? What impact could regularly-scheduled breaks for solitude have on your life and well-being? What ideas do you have for some mini-retreats of your own?

_____

 Rest Fit Tip:

To get on a healthy sleep schedule, set an alarm for your bedtime at night and avoid hitting the snooze button when you wake up in the morning.

SLEEP LIKE GOD'S BABY

Margaret Bentham-Moe

"So now I'll lie down and sleep like a baby—then I'll awake in safety, for you surround me with your glory."

~Psalms 3:5 (TPT)

Can we say that, in the midst of trouble, we sleep like a baby? When there's no pressing problem, per se, we can still find ourselves focusing on some issue. Our bodies may seemingly be in a restful position, but our minds, emotions, and souls are restless. What a stark contrast to David's state of mind in this Psalm, especially when we consider that he was running for his life, not just from outside enemies, but from his own son. He's actually out in the open and not in his palace laying on silk sheets.

What enabled him to truly rest despite his circumstances? He had made the decision to put his faith in God. Had David not trusted God to watch over him, instead of being at rest, he would have been consumed by anxiety.

There have been times, when worried about some circumstance, I couldn't sleep due to a bad case of the "what ifs." The hours ticked by and morning came; my lack of rest didn't change anything. How much happier I could have been had I made the decision, and yes, it's a decision, to simply trust God. I've come to realize that inability to be at rest is reflective of wavering faith and an unwillingness to wait on the Lord.

Hebrews 4:10 tells us that when we enter into God's rest we also rest from our own labors, just as God did after He created the world. We have to come to the realization that it's already done, and it is God who has done it. Having entered our homes, do we stand around wondering what it would be like to be inside; no, we are already in. When we receive Jesus as our Savior and Lord we must also enter into the finished work of the cross. Among the myriad of benefits to the believer, is rest. David was so confident of the *Rest of God* that he not only expected to sleep peacefully, he was also confident that—while he was at rest—no enemy could harm him and he would awake quite safe. God surrounded him with His Glory. We have that same assurance. Let's rest.

Father, You've given us the promise of entering into Your rest. By Your Grace we receive Your rest in every area of our lives. In Jesus Name.

Amen.

When was the last time you had a case of the "what ifs"? Did you eventually come around and decide to trust God? If so, how did that change your rest? If not, will you choose to trust Him and enter His rest today? Write your prayer to God.

_____

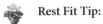 **Rest Fit Tip:**

Room temperature for optimum sleep should be between 60 and 67 degrees.

PERFECT PEACE

Tamara Fink

"You will keep in perfect peace those whose minds are steadfast, because they trust in you."

~Isaiah 26:3 (NIV)

What does your mind conjure up when you think of peace? A babbling brook? A calm mountain scene? A peaceful walk through the woods? Those places are nice, but I'm not slow and quiet! I talk fast! I pray fast! I journal fast!

I remember a time when I went on a silent prayer retreat. It was at a monastery way back in the woods. It was a beautiful, serene place with plenty of options for quiet get aways with God. I would be there for forty-eight hours; no talking, slowing my pace and no eye contact. Within twenty-four hours this sanguine girl thought she might explode. In a moment of complete desperation I started walking rather quickly down the long driveway. Pretty soon my brisk walk turned into an all out run. Running wasn't enough though, I began singing. Louder and louder until my spirit felt free. A peace washed over me that only another extrovert could understand. I asked God to forgive me for not being still, but I was pretty confident He was laughing with me because no forgiveness was needed. He hadn't made me to be quiet and slow.

What is peaceful for us may cause tension or unrest for someone else.

God's peace is perfect, it's without fault. It doesn't look a certain way that we must conform to. His peace is available to each of us at all times. God offers his perfect peace amidst the harshest storms; the affair revealed, the terrifying diagnosis from the doctor, the uncertain finances. There's never a time when we can't trust God. He is faithful. Our minds are what are not faithful. Our human tendency is to let our thoughts and emotions run amuck. Instead of letting our minds run in fear, let's set our thoughts on Him and His promises. Let Him run with your steadfast mind until you are singing louder and louder with Him.

Heavenly Father, I thank You that You offer perfect peace. Help me Lord to keep my thoughts immovable to Your perfect peace today.

Amen.

What are the runaway thoughts that you need to release to your trustworthy God? What are ways that you can recognize your emotions are running you instead of your steadfast mind?

___

 **Rest Fit Tip:**

A white-noise machine can aid in falling asleep.

Comfort In The Darkest Valleys

Kathy Thorsen

"The Lord is my shepherd, I shall not want. He makes me lie down in green pastures; he leads me beside still waters; He restores my soul. He leads me in right paths for his name's sake. Even though I walk through the valley of the shadow of death, I fear no evil, for You are with me; Your rod and Your staff, they comfort me."

~Psalm 23:1-4 (NASB)

There are 184 references to sheep in the Bible, thus indicating their importance. If we are like sheep to God, then we must also hold significance in his eyes. Why then do many of us feel like the lost sheep, searching for meaning, purpose and value in life? Perhaps it is the person who is always on the go, working, volunteering, or filling their time with activity, never stopping by the stream to replenish with water.

The sheep could also be like people who suffer from anxiety, depression and walk in the dark valley. Not all know the direction, steadfastness and inner peace that only He can offer. This was the case for my own niece who did not give herself a chance to rest in His loving care as she encountered a situation of dark despair. Instead of seeking counsel from Him or other loved ones, in 2017 she chose to depart this world at the age of twenty-six, leaving many behind to seek comfort and strength from His staff. When we rest in His loving care, it is easier to find patience, faith and hope during even the most difficult times while waiting for God to reveal His perfect plan one step at a time.

God ministers to all our needs if we rest our cares in His word. As our shepherd, He offers us provisions, restoration and strength. We in turn must quiet our minds and refrain from roaming down our own path, long enough to allow His guidance to penetrate our thoughts and direct our actions. *"Be still and know that I am God." (Psalm 46:10 NIV)* Though we may walk through treacherous terrain, where the unknown casts shadows of fear and doubt and are tempted to take a smoother route, the good shepherd will comfort, support and never leave us. He will lead us day by day down the right path as long as we focus our gaze on His guiding light.

My Shepherd, thank You for always providing everything I need and guiding me on this journey of life. Help me quiet my wandering thoughts and fears of tomorrow so that I may direct my mind and actions in accordance with Your will for me today.

Amen.

When you allow your mind or actions to wander from the direction indicated by your inner compass, do you turn to God to help get you back on track? Have you ever tried meditative breathing to reduce anxious thoughts? Take a moment and breathe deeply and slowly. Then release your anxious thoughts to the Lord right here:

_____

 Rest Fit Tip:

To prepare your mind and body for sleep, practice a relaxing bedtime ritual such as a bath or relaxation techniques.

New Creation From Transformation

Luanne Nelson

> "For in six days the LORD made the heavens and the earth, the sea, and all that is in them, but he rested on the seventh day. Therefore the LORD blessed the Sabbath day and made it holy."
>
> ~Exodus 20:11 (NIV)

God created the world and everything in it . . . all the physical stuff . . . in six days. And, on the seventh day, He continues to create us in the midst of resting. What we miss is that, unless we are still, He can't work on us. God did not need rest. What He's trying to say is 'You need to be still, because I'm not finished with you, yet.' Can you imagine if we were in charge of healing our own broken hearts and changing people's hearts around us? Only God, the Great Physician, can heal what we cannot see and heal what we are helpless to heal - which really, is everything.

"'But I will restore you to health and heal your wounds,' declares the Lord." (Jeremiah 30:17 NIV)

He is the only One who can heal us and change us. God not only wants us to rest on the seventh day, He also uses the day to show us how to be better versions of ourselves. He wants us to be still to receive his blessings and corrections. He is continuing to create each one of us, shaping us into the persons he wants us to become. What are the ways you rest and keep the Sabbath holy?

God not only wants us to rest on the seventh day, He wants us to realize he's blessed this day and made it holy. We recall not just the physical creation, but also remember the ongoing spiritual creation in each one of us. It's a holy time, set apart for God's use. Opening our hearts and spirits to receive divine holiness is not only about going to church and resting from work; rather, it's about opening ourselves to hearing His Word, prayerfully asking for forgiveness and cleansing - and putting the changes He puts into our hearts into action. This holy day of the week is the day He looks past our human nature and breathes the holy fire of His Spirit into our hearts. This is the day He changes us - shapes us into what He wants us to be. This is the day we rest in Him to become refreshed, renewed, forgiven, healed, and changed.

Father God, please make me new and improved. Forgive me and give me a new spotless heart filled with Your blessings. Make me holy. Please.

Amen.

Rest Of God

When we're used to constant movement and activity, it's difficult to actually stay still for more than a few minutes. How do you practice and perfect this holy exercise? God is asking us to be still for an entire day to open ourselves to receive his correction and blessings. He is asking us to be still so He can make us holy! He is calling us specifically on the seventh day to be with Him to become *Holy, Whole and Spiritually Fit*!

 Rest Fit Tip:

Avoid heavy meals late in the day; digestion can interfere with sleep.

GOD WHISPERS TO THE DESPERATE SOUL

Lisa Danegelis

> "The Lord is close to those who have a broken heart and saves those who have a contrite spirit."
>
> ~Psalms 34:18 (NKJV)

'The lowest part of the valley has the deepest wells,' I heard God's whisper as I headed for the couch in the wee hours of the morning.

I sensed Him drawing me into a time of intimacy which would help calm my shattered nerves and desperate soul. I was three years into the healing process after stopping the psychiatric drugs that had ravaged my mind and body. Severe insomnia was one of the many horrific symptoms I experienced. I was desperate. I was always desperate. I journaled these words His spirit invoked:

> "I know He is speaking of the wellsprings of life, of the solitude in the storm, the treasures in darkness. I feel the joy of suffering with Him, the level of surrender needed, the absolute trust in His goodness, the intimacy available. I feel a deeper love for Him than ever before, a knowing that my Daddy just can't do me wrong. A "Whatever God" I have never felt this deeply. I'm not sure how to explain it all, it's just a beautiful thing."

For years my prayers had been desperate, demanding, and whiny at best. I hadn't cracked open the Word in months. My soul was crushed, my faith all but gone. I felt as if I had failed Him. Yet here was my gracious God enrobing me in His compassion, saturating me in wisdom, and loving me in my mess.

When you find yourself in the night seasons of life, take comfort in the shadows. Growth happens slowly and effortlessly as a seed breaks forth with new life in the confines of dark soil. It rests and waits for its maker's timing, knowing it will soon spring up in brilliance. Find solace in your dark place friend, God is close and the well is abundant there.

Holy Spirit, thank You for comforting me in my brokenness. I trust that You will bring new life as I humbly wait on You.

Amen.

When the path is lonely and God feels distant, what may He whisper if you rested and listened for His voice? What treasures of darkness may you find? Sit with the Lord and ask Him to speak. Share your deepest pain with Him and then listen. Close your eyes, see yourself resting at His feet and wait for a thought, a verse, or a vision. Let His comfort saturate your soul.

 Rest Fit Tip:

Sleep deprivation can lead to heart disease, heart attack, high blood pressure, stroke, or diabetes.

HE IS OUR INFINITE STRENGTH

Tracy Hennes

"My health may fail, and my spirit may grow weak, but God remains the strength of my heart; he is mine forever."

~Psalms 73:26 (NLT)

I was staring at the creamy white ceiling again, striving just to breathe and stay awake. Every minute was a struggle for oxygen in spite of the elephant sitting on my chest. I would collect my strength and try to appear well whenever family and friends were present. I didn't want them to worry. As soon as they were out the door, I'd crawl back into bed, cry out to God, and sleep, restlessly. The pneumonia got worse and it took me months to recover. I had felt the failure of my body in a way I could not have imagined. As I was the usual caretaker in my home, I felt like there would be nobody to care for me. My work was coming home and piling up, adding to my stress. My body was shutting down, but I felt like my life would, too, if I stopped trying to push through. My life and my outlook would never be the same.

When I had no strength in my body or spirit, God was my strength. Have you or someone you love ever experienced a failure of the human body that the only choice left was to lean on God and others?

We are finite and weak, but God is infinitely strong. When we have no will left, His desire for us to thrive never waivers. Let God into your heart. Let Him be your strength. When others for ask for prayers, by all means, pray for them. Pray for God to enter their hearts and keep them strongly rooted in His love. Even though our bodies have an expiration date, our souls do not. We will leave the body behind, but the love in our heart lives on as part of our soul. Yes, we do still need to care for our bodies as cherished temples, but remember that they are not the most important component of who we are.

Rest in Him, knowing God's got our heart, soul, and strength, always and forever.

Dear Father, forever keeper of my heart, I praise You and thank You for being my strength when my will is weak and my body may fail me. I pray for those who may be experiencing failing health or weakness of will right now. I ask that they may lean into You and let You into their hearts. If it is Your will, Lord, please carry them through, and let their life glorify You.

Amen.

Have you experienced or witnessed an unimaginable failure in health? Describe the experience and the emotions of it here. When you reflect on that time, how was God there? If you know of someone(s) who could use your prayers to rest in God's strength, please write their name(s), say them aloud, and specifically pray for them right now. Lean into God and ask Him to provide strength for them.

Rest Fit Tip:

Improper sleep increases the risk of cardiovascular disease. Sleep helps the heart vessels to heal and rebuild. It also affects the processes that maintain blood pressure and inflammation control.

A Fruitful Rest

Kathy Thorsen

> "The Spirit of the LORD will rest on Him, The spirit of wisdom and understanding, The spirit of counsel and strength, The spirit of knowledge and the fear of the LORD."
>
> ~Isaiah 11:2 (NASB)

God created each of us with purpose and for a purpose. We all have a unique combination of characteristics developed both by environmental and intrinsic influences. When we are in flow with our gifts, it is as if we get where we need to go in a time capsule. Other days, it is as if we are driving through the same terrain for hours as we go about the mundane but necessary tasks to finish the day. It would be wonderful to receive a roadmap with every turn marked, to keep us moving smoothly on our journey, but God reveals each direction when we are ready, like the navigation system in our cars. God also gives us all the tools we need, in case our car breaks down, through the gifts of the Holy Spirit. The Book of Revelation describes the *"seven lamps of fire burning before the throne"* which alluded to the seven Spirits of God revealed throughout Jesus' mission as a human being. (Revelation 4:5)

Through confirmation of our belief, we have access to the fruit of the Spirit (Romans 8:23) that guided and supported Jesus on His earthly journey. The question for each of us is whether or not we choose to access these gifts and fulfill His purpose for our lives. Do we rest all our cares on Jesus and faithfully tend to the obligations He places in our path? When we look inward, He provides us with the spirit of wisdom to apply our knowledge, according to His will. Do we allow our childish nature to prevent the spirit of understanding, from helping us distinguish between good and evil? Because God knows our needs before we do, He is the ultimate Counselor to call on for direction. How often do we let fear drive us into a snowbank instead of calling on His spirit of strength to plow through life's greatest obstacles? God provides us with knowledge through resources more numerous than the features on a modern dashboard such as prayer, scripture, and church leaders, to name a few. Why, then, do we rely on our own knowledge when making decisions instead of calling on Jesus who knows our hearts, our minds, and our ways?

Through the fear of the Lord, we can believe in His power to overcome all evil. Then, we can rest in the truth that He is our God and we are His beloved children.

Thank You, God, for giving us the Gifts of the Holy Spirit so we may faithfully navigate this journey with Your help to utilize our talents according to Your plan.

Amen.

Who are you called to become? When was the last time you sought counsel from God regarding how you spend your days? What were you doing the last time you were in flow as though time stood still? Make a list of what you are passionate about? What fruit of the Spirit do you need to call upon to get closer to fulfilling the purpose God has dreamed for you?

Rest Fit Tip:

Hunger hormones, leptin and ghrelin, which control feelings of hunger and fullness, are affected by sleep.

WATER OF THE HOLY SPIRIT

It is estimated that the human body can survive little more than a week without water. It is no accident that God created us this way. He was demonstrating our desperate need for the **Water Of The Holy Spirit**.

Just like water cleanses, rejuvenates, and gives life to the human body, the Holy Spirit cleanses, rejuvenates, and gives life to the human heart. We first invite the Holy Spirit in upon our salvation, but we must continue to allow the Water of the Spirit to cleanse our souls or we will dry up and become lifeless.

There are seasons of drought in the world when water supplies dry up in certain regions . . . not so with the Water of the Spirit. It never runs out and is always poured out in abundance when we ask for more.

For "what man is there among you who, if his son asks for bread, will give him a stone? If you then, being evil, know how to give good gifts to your children, how much more will your Father who is in heaven give good things to those who ask Him!"

Our prayer is that you would ask our Heavenly Father today to pour out the Water of His Holy Spirit on every dry place in your heart, and that you would continue to drink Him in, all the days of your life.

THE WORD SPIRITUALLY CLEANSES

Margaret Bentham-Moe

> "I will bring some water to wash your feet. You can rest under the trees."
> ~Genesis 18:4 (ERV)

Have you ever visited someone and were offered water to wash your feet? To Abraham, this was basic hospitality. The culture of the time expected such to be done. We see that in *Luke 7:44 – Jesus upbraided Simon for his failure to perform this act of welcoming, Jesus said to him 'When I came into your house, you gave Me no water for My feet.'"* Roads were not paved as they are today; people walked to most places wearing sandals, so naturally their feet became dusty.

Apart from this physical significance of washing with water, the Word of God and the Holy Spirit Himself is referred to as water. It's easy to see why God does this. We understand that water cleanses, refreshes, and preserves life and medical experts even recommend certain daily quantities of water, but the Word of God has the power to cleanse and bring life to our souls. God's Word removes what the purest springs on earth cannot.

Isaiah 12:13 speaks of drawing water from the wells of salvation. Jesus in John 4:10 spoke to the woman at the well of living water, which is the answer to thirst itself and that He is the source of this water. Paul, in *Ephesians 5:26-27*, speaks of Jesus' ultimate cleansing of the Church, *"by the washing of water by the Word so that He could present it to himself, glorious without spot or wrinkle, holy and without blemish."*

The correlation between physical cleansing with water and the power of the Word of God to cleanse spiritually shows us how God uses His word to deal with our inner man. Jesus washed the disciples' feet and here we have a humbling and literal example of the Word, who is Jesus, washing away the dust and mire we accumulate as we walk through life. Once we receive salvation, the water of the word is now for our sanctification and it is for this reason that we need to fill up on the scriptures daily.

Father, we know of our need for water to preserve life itself and to keep our physical bodies clean. By Your grace let us be cognizant of the fact that You have also made Your Word water for us and it is the only thing with the power to address the thirsting of our souls.

Amen.

Water Of The Holy Spirit

What is something that leaves your feet "dusty" each day from walking your own road? Ask the Holy Spirit to wash you today. Invite Him to satisfy your thirst and then thank Him for His never-condemning-love, poured out like water!

 Water Fit Tip:

It's a fact: drinking water is essential to our being. We must drink water to stay hydrated and replenish the water that we lose throughout the day.

Drink In His Love

Tamara Fink

Now on the last day, the great day of the feast, Jesus stood and cried out, saying, "If anyone is thirsty, let him come to Me and drink.

~John 7:37 (NIV)

My drink of choice had been Diet Coke™ for a long time. I started drinking it years ago when I was trying to lose weight and wanted something sweet that didn't have calories. It was a rare treat. Over time it became something I enjoyed with my pizza, chips, and salsa. Then I realized it was a good pick-me-up in the morning and at that 3:00 lull in the afternoon. In a short amount of time, I had taken something that was a rare treat and made it part of my daily consumption on an extremely unhealthy level. As I realized how this unhealthy choice was affecting me, I tried to stop drinking it, but I had created a dependency on it. It had become my drink to unwind, celebrate, console, encourage, ease boredom, and wake me up. It became something that I relied on without even realizing it.

Have you ever leaned on something unhealthy? Created a dependency on something to help you get through your day or through an event? This is precisely why Jesus is calling us onto Himself. He knows we were each created with an unquenchable thirst. That thirst was meant to be a desire for more of Him. Think about your thirst for water. Our bodies need to be refreshed continually everyday with water. Just like our physical body's need for water, so is our spiritual man in need of God every day, all day. My dependency on Diet Coke™ to soothe me or encourage me always left me wanting for something more. Not only was my physical thirst not quenched, neither was the deeper desire I was trying to mask. Jesus is the source of all satisfaction. When we drink in His love and receive his salvation He offers us abundant life.

Lord Jesus, I thank You that You are the Living Water and that you satisfy my every need. Please help me to remember that You are what I need to be drinking in. Everything else will leave me wanting.

Amen.

WATER OF THE HOLY SPIRIT

What are you drinking from to meet your emotional need? How can you begin to replace that "water" with the life-giving water of Christ?

Water Fit Tip:

Give up soda and juices that contain a lot of sugar and replace them with sparkling or mineral water.

DRAW FROM THE FULL POTENTIAL OF THE WATER OF THE SPIRIT

Candice Moe

"Oh, the joys of those who do not follow the advice of the wicked, or stand around with sinners, or join in with mockers. But they delight in the law of the Lord, meditating on it day and night. They are like trees planted along the riverbank, bearing fruit each season. Their leaves never wither, and they prosper in all they do."

~Psalms 1:1-3 (NLT)

A riverbank is defined as the land at the water's edge. "Land" reminds us of the verse shared at memorials that says, *"from dust you came and to dust you shall return."* At the risk of sounding morbid, I submit to you that you are that dust, that land, lovingly situated alongside Holy Spirit. *"(We) are (also) like trees planted along the riverbank (that land!), bearing fruit each season."*

The third Person of the Trinity, was eagerly awaited by believers of Biblical times because Jesus promised to ask The Father to Gift Him to the church for all generations (Acts 2:26 KJV). At Pentecost, Holy Spirit relocated to earth, bringing with Him gifts and fruit available for the asking. Jesus said in *John 16:7 TPT, "But here's the Truth: It's to your advantage that I go away, for if I don't go away the Divine Encourager will not be released to you. But after I depart, I will send Him to you."* Your Divine Encourager desires to pilot, coach, embolden and invigorate you. In botany, evergreen trees never relinquish all their foliage adjusting to changing seasons but jettison their leaves gradually. Similarly, Holy Spirit is patient, endeavoring to refine us incrementally, rather than overwhelm us with haste.

Trees are typically identified by their fruit. For example, orange trees yield oranges. Apple trees bring forth apples. A banana bears from a banana tree. We to are known by our fruit (Luke 6:43-45). Drinking liberally from Holy Spirit's Living Water, you'll re-produce love, joy, peace, patience, goodness, faith, humility, gentleness, and self-control. Unreservedly submerge your roots into His riverbank during the fluctuating seasons of life. Acclimatize to Heaven and thus perpetually produce much fruit. Adjacent deciduous trees will perceive your Heavenly Father's glory as your leaves remain inoculated and your branches laden with succulent fruit.

Shelter provided by existing evergreen plants foster survival of younger evergreens during cold and drought. Are you providing spiritual shelter for family and friends? Jesus offers you an infallible formula. *"In the same way, you should be a Light for other people. Live so that they will see the good things you do. Live so that they will Praise your Father in Heaven."* (Matthew 5:16 ICB)

Jesus, thank You for Your Gift of Holy Spirit. I receive Him into my life and look forward to a deepening relationship, producing much fruit. Help me to cast my burdens on You so that I'm able to effectively shine. I declare the salvation of those around me and praise You in advance. *Amen.*

Water Of The Holy Spirit

The fruit of the Spirit is the full potential available to you, right now! What would you say are the "fruits" you most commonly bear? What fruits of the Spirit would you like to replace your typical fruits with? Are you a tree planted by the riverbank? What can you do to stay rooted in the Water of the Spirit?

_____
_____
_____
_____
_____
_____
_____
_____
_____
_____
_____
_____
_____
_____
_____
_____
_____
_____
_____

Water Fit Tip:

Water consumption is a key component in your weight loss strategy. It increases the rate of fat-burning and eliminates fat cells from the body.

HIS LOVE POURED OUT WITH PAIN

Rebecca Grambort

> "Not only so, but we also glory in our sufferings, because we know that suffering produces perseverance; perseverance, character; and character, hope. And hope does not put us to shame, because God's love has been poured out into our hearts through the Holy Spirit, who has been given to us."
>
> ~Romans 5:3-4 (NIV)

When reading a verse, have you ever pondered, 'What does the author know that I don't?' In this writing, Paul knows that suffering produces perseverance and from that character is produced and so on. It might seem obvious that he is speaking from experience yet, from my lack thereof, I can say that I previously could not understand what Paul so clearly did. It wasn't until later through my own tribulations would I be able to connect the dots . . . from my head . . . to my heart.

Suffering can cause us to struggle in a way that can seem unbearable at times. Nevertheless, it is useful tool that can lead to accomplishing an end result. When you were young, you struggled to ride a bike; you struggled to learn to read. Your parents refused to give in to your complaints, knowing that your efforts would eventually pay off. They couldn't do it for you. These struggles belonged to you, and only you held the power to earn your reward. Over time, you mastered these skills and you suddenly performed them with such ease that they became second-nature. In hindsight, we can see that these struggles were a gift. Without them, one would be ill-equipped for what lay ahead.

We should view our sufferings in the same light as the struggles that come with childhood learning. Suffering leads us to encountering Jesus, the only One who can give us a true and everlasting hope. And so, to glory should be our stance no matter what our temporary circumstances bring. Let's remember, not all gifts come wrapped in pretty packages. God doesn't just pour out His love to us through the free gift of the Holy Spirit (that came with a price); but also through gifts disguised as suffering (that come with a price). These loving gifts are the assurant hope that will never put us to shame.

Lord, help me to glory in my sufferings knowing that this pain produces a change in me that will be used for my good and for Your Glory.

Amen.

When we understand that our sufferings produce Heavenly gain later, perseverance will come naturally, now. This gives us the Christ-like character to help us hold still on the potter's wheel as He shapes us into His image. In what ways can you decide to glory in your sufferings? In what ways can you decide to use your pain usefully instead of letting it use you?

_____

_____

_____

_____

_____

_____

_____

_____

_____

_____

_____

_____

_____

_____

_____

_____

_____

_____

_____

_____

Water Fit Tip:

Even mild dehydration can greatly affect your brain, potentially causing anxiety, memory-loss, and increased headaches. Drinking a healthy amount of water throughout the day is key.

GOD WANTS US TO DRINK JESUS' WATER, THE HOLY SPIRIT

Danelle Skinner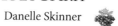

"Jesus said, 'Everyone who drinks this water will get thirsty again and again. Anyone who drinks the water I give will never thirst—not ever. The water I give will be an artesian spring within, gushing fountains of endless life.'"

~John 4:13-14 (MSG)

Are you thirsty, longing for something and are never satisfied? Maybe you've searched for happiness, security and satisfaction in worldly things, only to leave you thirsty for more again and again? Finding yourself empty and unfulfilled? Jesus said to them, *"Very truly I tell you, unless you eat the flesh of the Son of Man and drink his blood, you have no life in you." (John 6:53 New NIV)*

I found myself there after having my children. They are blessings from the Lord and this was in no way their fault, but I lost my worldly identity after having them. Everything changed. My career was put on hold, my friendships changed, and things that used to make me happy completely stopped quenching my thirst for happiness. I was so thirsty, unfilled, and empty. My identity as I knew it was gone and I felt as though I had no life in me, until I started drinking Jesus' water by reading the Bible and focusing on His presence, the Holy Spirit. It was then I found my identity in Christ. He made me no longer empty, searching, and thirsty.

Jesus' water, the Holy Spirit, quenches our thirst . . . like an Artisan spring, a well that produces a constant supply of water. This means if we seek the Lord and drink of His water we will never thirst. Like the Artisan spring, the Holy Spirit constantly supplies water. What is water? In our physical life, water cleanses and purifies. Likewise, in our spiritual lives, the Holy Spirit is constantly at work to baptize, cleanse, and purify us. Have you invited the Holy Spirit to do His work in you? If spiritual health is our focus, a focus of cultivating health and wellness in Christ. The Holy Spirit will organically transform us from the inside out until our thoughts and desires are more in-line with Christ, who is *Holy, Whole, and Fit.*

God offers eternal life, lacking in nothing, if you drink His water.

Lord, thank You for sending the Holy Spirit to do Your work in me, transforming me little by little to become more like Your Son, Jesus. Lord please baptize me, cleanse my soul, and purify my heart.

Amen.

What are the worldly things you drink that are leaving you thirsty again and again? Imagine drinking Jesus' water, the Holy Spirit, allowing Him to cleanse and purify you. What would your life look like if your thirst was quenched . . . forever?

 Rest Fit Tip:

Reward yourself in a healthy way for getting your water ounces in each day.

MOVING WATER

Tracy Hennes

> "Dear friend, I hope all is well with you and that you are as healthy in body as you are strong in spirit."
>
> ~3 John 1:2 (NLT)

I hear the resonance of water rushing in an airy white curtain over the rocks and splashing as it lands many feet below before it continues onward and downward. For as long as I can remember, I've loved hiking up into the hills and mountains to see streams and waterfalls. The beauty, power, persistence of water as it finds a way over, around, and through land and rock is something I could never tire of. Many would argue that there is no substance on earth as strong and powerful as water. One thing is for sure, when water is moving, it will eventually find a way. How do you see the power of the Holy Spirit as similar to the power of water?

When we read 3 John 1:2, we are reminded that—as a friend to Jesus—we are loved. He wants our body to be as healthy, as the power of the Holy Spirit in us is strong. That's huge! The life-giving energy of the Holy Spirit is the strongest force within us. It shapes who we are and, at any given moment, is capable of overcoming any imperfection within us to make us new. When we think of the powers of water and the Holy Spirit, both are life-giving, life-sustaining, cleansing, flowing, nourishing, persisting, obstacle bending, soft, and fluid, yet tough enough to cut through rock. Now that's powerful and God wants our bodily health to be just as powerfully strong! It's no wonder God designed the human body to made mostly of water. He makes no mistakes. We are physically powered by water and spiritually powered by the life-giving *Water of the Holy Spirit*.

God, thank You for Your amazing design of the human body. I am sorry for the times I have taken my God-given power for granted. Please help me, Lord, to honor Your love and Your desire for me to be healthy and strong in body and spirit.

Amen.

Water Of The Holy Spirit

What do you see when you picture what the power of moving water can do to anything that comes in its way... a log, a rock, an embankment? Now imagine that *Water of the Holy Spirit* washing over the debris of your life. What rough edges, logs, and rocks would you like to invite the Holy Spirit to wash over so that you can be healthy in body and strong in spirit?

Water Fit Tip:

Drinking a glass or two of water in the mornings when you rise stimulates metabolism and provides mental clarity.

God Wants Us To Call On Him

Danelle Skinner

"But you received the Holy Spirit. He lives within you, you don't need anyone to teach you what is true. What He teaches is true – it is not a lie. So just as He has taught you remain in fellowship with Christ."

~1 John 2:27 (NLT)

Have you ever had a day where you thought, if one more thing happens, I don't think I'm going to survive? I had a day like that once. I was off balance from the moment I woke, and apparently the kids were too. We struggled to get ready for school, there was screaming, fighting, and crying. I misplaced my keys, we were late, and my son forgot he set his snack down at home. The day continued rushed and I received devastating news from my doctor; I could no longer hold my tears back. It was date night with my husband and we found he was as behind as us. We settled to forgo dinner and meet at a theater in the middle. We planned to eat there. Realizing the theater did not have food, I rushed elsewhere to grab dinner and stumbled on a pothole, then tripped and fell – hard! I honestly wasn't sure I could physically and spiritually get up. There were rocks in my hands, bloody scrapes on my knees, and pain in my wrists. My first thought was to call my friend. At that moment, I felt an intense tug on my heart. "You asked me to tell you what you are doing wrong. How can she help you? She is not here. I am here! Right here, right now I am with you! I can help you stand up!" I felt Him invite me to call on Him, not on my friends, Him. I knew what He was teaching me. It was more comfortable for me to ask my friends to pray for me than to pray for myself.

I am thankful the Holy Spirit is not something we have to purchase or earn and equally thankful it is not something we can lose. It is a gift given to all believers at the cross. He teaches us truth, because everything He is, is truth. He does not deceive as the world deceives because He is not of this world. He is God's truth and He knows our truth. He is our own personal spiritual guide, teaching us through life's journey. What a gift! Each day He lays out hidden treasures, strategically-placed to teach and grow us to be more like Jesus, cultivating our hearts from the inside out for a harvest. He also blesses us along the way, revealing His presence in us. Showing we are not alone. His availability is instant. No phone call required. Sure, it is comforting to know our friends are a phone call away. It is even more comforting to know the Holy Spirit is with us, even when we fall. He wants to be in fellowship with us. He wants us to call on Him. When I read the Bible, I hear Him saying, when life doesn't add up, you can count on me. When you're low, you can come get high on me. When you're exhausted, you can come to rest in me. When things get heavy, you can put the weight on me. When you're mad, you can give your anger to me. Daughter, call on me, put it all on me! I'm here for you even when you fall! He helped me stand up that day and many days since. Knowing He is with me, even when I fall, has given me an unexplainable peace.

Dear God, thank You for being readily available for me to call on You. Thank You for using little things along the way to reveal the Holy Spirit's presence. Please help me to recognize the treasures set aside for me to grow, teaching me to be more like Your Son, Jesus Christ.   *Amen.*

God is with you every moment; call on him. Do you recognize where the Holy Spirit is currently teaching and growing you? Have there been blessings along the way revealing His presence in you? Journal about how you call on the Lord.

Water Fit Tip:

Set multiple alarms on your smartphone to remind yourself to drink water throughout your day.

WASHING FOR THE GREATER GOOD

Rebecca Grambort

"Wash yourselves; make yourselves clean; remove the evil of your deeds from before my eyes; cease to do evil, learn to do good; seek justice, correct oppression; bring justice to the fatherless, plead the widow's cause."

~Isaiah 1:16-17 (ESV)

Wash yourself with the Word. Let the Spirit's words pour over your mind, will, and emotions. Repeat this process often, because living in a world full of all kinds of evil can make you filthy in a hurry. His words will not only wash you, but the precious blood of Jesus will also make you clean. As you wash yourself regularly, also keep in continual repentance. In doing so, you will learn His ways which are always to do good. This will help you to turn away from your former deeds so that you do not add to this world's oppression. Do what you can to come alongside the fatherless and petition for the widows in need. In these ways, you partner with Heaven to get this holy work done.

God is vigilantly aware that many of His children have been treated unjustly. His precious son was also mistreated by the world. Keep in mind that they know not what they do. Be quick to forgive and turn them over to God, remembering that you are not their judge. Only God can see the heart and He is slow to anger so that everyone has a chance to receive His gift of repentance. Sit down in your rightful seat of forgiveness with trust, remembering always that He is the Good Judge. While you are waiting, you will have your hands full with your own work of keeping yourself clean and helping others. Trust Your Father as the Good Judge to do the rest. When you realize that The Judge is also Your Father you will be confident that His ruling is in your favor!

Father, as I wait for You to correct the oppression that afflicts this world, I will do my part to keep washing myself clean so that I do not add to this world's injustices. Thank You that as your child, I can be confident that You rule in our favor!

Amen.

In a world filled with evil and injustice it can be hard to keep clean. Let God's justice pour over your entire being knowing that He is ultimately in control. Let this thought flood you with the peace that these afflictions are temporary and that oppression will be completely corrected in Heaven. Can you think of some ways that you can keep yourself clean - mind, body and soul? Journal your ideas below.

Rest Fit Tip:

Proper hydration promotes digestion and can prevent constipation. Water consumption boosts metabolism so you can properly breakdown your food.

GO BIG

Jane Guffy

"'It shall come to pass that before they call, I will answer; and while they are still speaking, I will hear.' And in the fourth watch of the night he came to them, walking on the sea. But when the disciples saw him walking on the sea, they were terrified, and said, 'It is a ghost!' and they cried out in fear. But immediately Jesus spoke to them, saying, 'Take heart; it is I. Do not be afraid.' And Peter answered him, 'Lord, if it is you, command me to come to you on the water.' He said, 'Come.' So Peter got out of the boat and walked on the water and came to Jesus.'"

~Matthew 14:25-29 (NIV)

Water elicits a natural response from all of us. My family loves playing in and around the water! When I walk at the marina, I enjoy the slapping of water on the rocking boats with their weathered ropes tying them the stability of a pier. The sound of the sea drowns out my voice! Water at night is daunting; I don't like the limited visibility of the unknown. Nearby light from shores and towns adds a glow to our night skies . . . that was not the case with Peter and his crew. At the time of fourth watch, they may have been lulled into a half sleep. The sound of water is familiar to each of us. It's the sound our babies hear in utero, when they are connected and protected to their source of life, anchored in stability. God brings us into the world after being surround by water! Soon-to-be mothers learn of pending delivery when their waters break. The element of surprise coming to you from the water.

Jesus came to them walking on the sea, at night. He was defying gravity, which scared them. His words were meant to calm their fears.

He said, *"It is I."*

Certainly, Peter recognized his voice, but needed more. I get that! He wanted a miracle! *"Command me to come to you on the water."* Peter said on the water.

He wanted to do it Jesus' way, not his way. Peter didn't ask to be asked, he said "Command me" - he went big! Jesus did big right back! Only Jesus can approach from the sea yet test the depths of our faith.

Thank You, God, for always being big, answering us, reassuring us, and calming our fears. Thank You for stepping out onto the waters you created in the storms that we make, in order to save us.

Amen.

How many times have you asked for the big and received it? To what end? What waters have you walked on to meet Jesus?

 Water Fit Tip:

Dehydration can also seem like hunger and lead to unnecessary snacking. Before you take a bite, take a drink!

CALLED TO IGNITE YOUR SPIRITUAL GIFTS

Kathy Thorsen

"For this reason I remind you to rekindle the gift of God that is within you through the laying on of my hands; for God did not give us a spirit of cowardice, but rather a spirit of power and of love and of self-discipline."
~2 Timothy 1:7 (NRSV)

When I am asked to speak in front of adults, play the piano, or sing to an unfamiliar audience; my heart races, hands become sweaty, and sometimes feel my body and brain freeze like a scared deer looking into the headlights. Then, the whispers of the antagonist resonate in my mind as I say to myself, 'I'm not good at public speaking. What if I mess up the notes or my voice cracks?'

At that moment, the fire kindled by my God-given talents, preparation, and practice is put out like a bucket of water quenching a campfire. Then, I dig deep into my core and call on the Holy Spirit to dispel these toxic thoughts and remind myself that I am a beloved child of God who can face uncomfortable situations with His help. This is where power and love penetrate to override negative thinking. The more I consciously connect with my thoughts and allow the power of God's Spirit to fill my mind, the more my subconscious allows for positive outcomes that align with God's plan.

God calls us through thoughtful discipline to bravely ignite our spiritual gifts. God created each one of us to do great things; whether they seem small or large, within our comfort zone, or in uncharted territory. This requires us to call on the Holy Spirit to choose only powerful and loving thoughts to permeate our subconscious and direct our perceptions. We cannot allow fear to put out His fire, thus paralyzing our spirit, soul, and body. Only by drawing closer to God in prayer and practicing discipline in reprogramming limiting thoughts, will we be able to control our reactions and actions in life circumstances according to His plan.

God, thank You for the free will to control my thoughts. Forgive me for all the times where I allowed negative, self-limiting beliefs to prevent me from doing Your will. I ask that You help me execute self-discipline by inviting the Holy Spirit into my mind when I am faced with a difficult situation so that I may act with power and love to do what is pleasing to You.

Amen.

What uncomfortable tasks or situations are you being called to face, but from which you hesitate or run away because of your own limiting thoughts? What gifts has God given you and how often do you use them to serve Him?

_____
_____
_____
_____
_____
_____
_____
_____
_____
_____
_____
_____
_____
_____
_____
_____
_____
_____
_____
_____
_____

 Water Fit Tip:

To determine the number of ounces of water your body needs each day, divide your weight in half and drink that in ounces.

Those Pesky Paradoxes In Life

Luanne Nelson

On the same day, when evening had come, He said to them, "Let us cross over to the other side." Now when they had left the multitude, they took Him along in the boat as He was. And other little boats were also with Him. And a great windstorm arose, and the waves beat into the boat, so that it was already filling. But He was in the stern, asleep on a pillow. And they awoke Him and said to Him, "Teacher, do You not care that we are perishing?" Then He arose and rebuked the wind, and said to the sea, "Peace, be still!" And the wind ceased and there was a great calm. But He said to them, "Why are you so fearful? How is it that you have no faith?" And they feared exceedingly, and said to one another, "Who can this be, that even the wind and the sea obey Him!"

~Mark 4:35-41 (NKJV)

It's one of the paradoxes that keeps me wondering. Water is cleansing. Water is thirst-quenching. Our bodies are over sixty-five percent water. Yet, too much water can kill. Water the life-giver. Water the murderer. I've lived next to a creek, a river, a lake, and an ocean. The roars and thunderous claps of the water, the gentle ebb and flow, the beauty of it all, the terror of it all. My body can live without food for weeks; without water, I am delirious within days and dead in a week. If I don't stay hydrated while I am working out, I cramp and fizzle; too much water and I feel nauseous. What contradiction in your life keeps you awake at night?

This parable from Mark 4 is all about faith over fear. It's about faith over the terrifying reality of near capsizing and drowning. It's interesting to notice Jesus suggested the boat trip to his friends and then He fell sound asleep almost immediately. If they truly had faith, they would not have awakened Him. We all have storms in our lives. We can rest in faith because Jesus is on board; our boat is not going down. He commands wind, waves, and water. Everything. Every single thing. It is with this blind faith, this complete trust, we know we will not drown.

Father God, thank You for calming the most confounding paradoxes we come up with and loving us so much anyway.

Amen.

Water Of The Holy Spirit

Water brings baptism to our new life in Jesus Christ! Water is hydration! Water is a daily gift we often take for granted; another paradox. Challenge yourself to be aware of the clean, replenishing, life-saving water you use today. List the ways you receive this free-flowing gift and think of ways you can use it to serve others through Christ.

_____

Water Fit Tip:

Skin is 64% water, so the absence of water will leave wrinkles more pronounced and pores more prominent. If you want to give your skin the best chance it has against aging, free radicals, and sun damage, drink more water!

LIKE A NEW PERSON

Marlene Dawson

"As [John] preached he said, 'The real action comes next: the star in this drama, to who I'm a mere stagehand, will change your life. I'm baptizing you here in the river, turning your old life in for a kingdom life. His baptism – a holy baptism by the Holy Spirit – will change you from the inside out.'"

~Mark 1:7-8 (MSG)

I remember my husband arriving from work after a hot, sweaty day, wanting a shower. Afterward, he always exclaimed, "I feel like a new man!" There were also many showers taken to wash off the sand we brought from the beach, or ball games, or just the kids. Water can be restorative when it rids us of the dirt and grime of life, be it a shower, a pool, or a river. In each of these circumstances the water cleans us. I think God may have chosen water as the vehicle for baptism because we can all relate to that feeling of newness we get from being clean.

When Mark quotes John in chapter 1:7-8, we learn that water baptism is the evidence that we have accepted Jesus' love filled offer, called the "divine exchange." This is when God exchanges His holiness and righteousness for our sin and brokenness. When we are baptized in water, we are telling everyone that we have repented of our sin and are now followers of God. Then there is the baptism in the Holy Spirit. Acts 1:8 informs us this baptism is for believers to have the power of God manifested so He can flow directly through our lives. This is how we can become "like a new person!"

Thank You, God, for Your divine exchange . . . for making us clean and new. I ask You to flow through my new Kingdom life that it may be used for Your Glory.

Amen.

Water Of The Holy Spirit

Baptism, or being born again as some denominations call the experience, is a one-time event in our lives. Think of a time when the enemy attempted to convince you that your experience was not real. How did you put this lie to rest? How have you been able to use this to encourage another believer to hold tight to God in the difficult times of life?

_____
_____
_____
_____
_____
_____
_____
_____
_____
_____
_____
_____
_____
_____
_____
_____
_____
_____
_____
_____

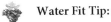 **Water Fit Tip:**

Drinking hot water in the morning aids in digestion and at night, aids in relaxation.

FREE

Kathy Carter

"I waited patiently for the Lord; and He inclined to me, and heard my cry. He also brought me up out of a horrible pit, out of the miry clay, and set my feet upon a rock, and established my steps."

~1 Corinthians 6:11 (CSB)

Free! What does that word mean to you? Over the years my definition has changed immensely. As a child I thought free meant to run in the fields and play, "carefree," away from chores, homework, and routine. As a teen moving into young adulthood, I felt free when I was released from my parents' rules, making my own decisions . . . whether the right ones or not, they were my own! When I reflect on those years, they made me who I am today.

Unfortunately, sometimes we dwell on those not-so-good choices from the past, lock them up in a box in our memory and think they will forever be forgotten. We may not think about them for a long time, but they are never truly gone. Oftentimes, those poor choices end up defining us with shame and feelings of unworthiness to a point where we forget who we are in God's eyes.

This negative dwelling was my experience for over thirty years until recently when I attended a Christian retreat to restore and refresh my soul. Never did I feel closer and safer in a room full of women than I did there. Never had I felt closer to God's presence than I did that weekend. I finally let go of that locked up box inside of me that had been full of shame and regret. I gave it all to God and He told me to forgive myself as He has forgiven me. He had washed me clean with his blood years ago. There at the conference free meant to release the chains that bound me for so long. There I became free to be God's child again, His bride and His beloved.

In 1 Corinthians 6:11, the Corinthians are warned against many great evils of which they had formerly been guilty. They are reminded of the power of the gospel and of the grace of God. The blood of Christ can wash away sins and take away all guilt. The gospel will change lives even in the face of overwhelming odds.

Dear God, thank You for sacrificing Your Son to wash away our sins and to set us free from the chains we carry from our pasts. Help us to focus on Your grace and each new day. In Your name, Jesus Christ.

Amen.

WATER OF THE HOLY SPIRIT

Have you ever been trapped by unexpressed feelings? Imagine an existence free from judgment for your past emotions and experiences. Imagine the freedom of vulnerability because you are in the safety of God's environment. If you believed you were unconditionally loved by God, no matter what you released in the world, how would you change the way you dealt with regret or past mistakes?

 **Water Fit Tip:**

To improve the taste of water, add lemons, limes, berries, or cucumbers.

YOU ARE PERFECT IN HIS HOLY SPIRIT

Luanne Nelson

That He might sanctify and cleanse her with the washing of water by the word.
~Ephesians 5:26 (NKJV)

The first time I heard I was supposed to love my body, I thought the notion was ridiculous. My feet are flat as a duck's and my knees dislocate on an ice cube. The list of imperfections goes on and on. I was always last on the bench to be picked for a team. I knew the marriage between contact sports and this body of mine was never going to be a successful one. It was later in life I realized that physical endurance came in many forms. Even if I could not compete in organized sports, I could run the race within myself and still achieve a personal best. After all, my body is the Temple of the Holy Spirit and God knew what He was doing when He gave me this one *(1 Corinthians 6:19-20 – "Or do you not know that your body is the temple of the Holy Spirit who is in you, whom you have from God, and you are not your own?")*

I've learned I feel best when I strengthen my body; I feel joy when I push myself to the limit, reaching new heights. What prevents you from reaching joyous heights?

God knows we are not all the same when we are running the race. He knows our strengths. If we can't run laps and jump hurdles, we can discover exercises that will strengthen and challenge us. But how do we maintain that strength? Replenishment doesn't happen on its own. Our spirits thirst for replenishment as much as our bodies do. We rejuvenate and make ourselves holy by reading the Word. We are strengthened, cleansed, and purified every time by this holy watering of His Word. Wearing our personal best body and Spirit, we present ourselves to our Creator - our bodies strengthened and our spirits cleansed and purified by the water of His word.

God lives in us by His Holy Spirit. We are challenged to honor and glorify God with our bodies; each one of us becomes His Holy Temple here on earth at baptism by water. No matter how you look at your physical appearance, you must remember this: You are made holy, precious, and perfect because the King of Glory has made His home in you through the Holy Spirit!

Father God, thank You for this body you have given me to wear in this life and this Spirit You have breathed into me. I pray that I am clean enough in both body and Spirit to stand before You someday in joy and thanksgiving without embarrassment, shame, or excuses.

Amen.

WATER OF THE HOLY SPIRIT

Take a moment to recall and write about the things you thought were physical defects. Then, write about how God has used these parts of your body and Spirit for his Glory!

Water Fit Tip:

Drinking more water can aid in weight loss, manage diabetes, essential in pregnancy and also keeps your teeth, skin and gums healthy.

A Promise For Your Family

Kimberly Joy Krueger

"For I will pour water on the thirsty ground and send streams coursing through the parched earth. I will pour my Spirit into your descendants and my blessing on your children."

~Isaiah 44:3 (MSG)

When I was a young mother of many, I was learning to serve God, homeschooling, and trying to be a godly wife. All the while, I was neck-deep in the cycle of co-dependency. I loved Jesus, but I was an enabler. I covered up for and rescued a loved one who was addicted . . . for years. At first, it felt good; like I was really "helping." When things got worse, not better, the good feelings dried up like the dry, parched ground Isaiah speaks of.

The tricky thing about co-dependency is that it does start out with some life, some vegetation, and even some beauty. Though as the cycle continues, the uglier, dryer, and more lifeless you become. The ground of my heart was so dry, it was brittle. I was a resentful, controlling, self-pitiful woman and I needed the Water of the Spirit to end my drought—desperately. I cried out, and His Water flowed; it began to quench my thirst and I couldn't get enough. I was ready for the truth and I could finally see the anger, fear, and lies for what they really were; a cancer that was spreading to my whole family. Was it too late for my children?

I didn't fully understand the Promise in Isaiah 44 then, but I knew that I could only change my own role in this tired old play. With all the courage I could muster, I started to read from a new script and refused to appear on that old victim's stage. That was almost twenty years ago and I am delighted to say that the tide has turned, not just for me, but for my family, too! When the streams of the Spirit course through your life, they will reach your children!

Now there are days we can actually be mistaken for a normal family, instead of an episode of "Jerry Springer!" We are learning to really love each other. I've even watched my kids break patterns that took me forty years to conquer. I've been amazed at how far we've come and the blessings we now enjoy, against all odds.

I recently heard a sermon about dysfunctional families. The pastor said, "To put an end to dysfunctional patterns, it requires a dramatic intervention." That is when it hit me—that is exactly what the *Water of the Holy Spirit* did for us . . . and He can do it for you and your family, too!

Holy Spirit, open the floodgates of Your Spirit to pour out and fill every crack and crevice in my heart, life, and family! May blessing flow in the place of every unhealthy pattern as you bless my children.

Amen.

WATER OF THE HOLY SPIRIT

What are the dry places in your heart that are thirsty for the Water of the Spirit? Can you identify unhealthy patterns in any of your relationships? What do they look like and how are they affecting you? Ask the Holy Spirit to flow to each unhealthy pattern in your life.

_____
_____
_____
_____
_____
_____
_____
_____
_____
_____
_____
_____
_____
_____
_____
_____
_____
_____
_____
_____

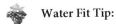 **Water Fit Tip:**

Create a deadline for your water drinking. Meet your water goal by the end of the workday.

Abundance In The Storm

Lisa Danegelis

"For the mountains shall depart and the hills be removed, but my kindness shall not depart from you."

~Isaiah 54:4 NKJV

A new believer often sees God through rose-colored glasses, ready to bless and eager to answer every prayer. After all, He does say He will give us abundant life. What else could that mean but a life brimming with happiness? That was once my limited view. I was expecting an occasional raindrop of pain in a sea of grace. I did not yet understand the wealth of an inner abundance. The tides of my life turned, the boat rocked, and a violent storm raged . . . a storm that seemed to know no end. That is when I started to look for raindrops of grace in my sea of pain. The God who had immersed me in His presence, spoke to me passionately, and blessed my every move, had become silent and distant. As wave after merciless wave crashed over me, I desperately searched for my beloved Lord. I learned to search for Him in the storm. The storm He approved.

God once told me, "Do not despise the quiet dark days, all days are good in My presence."

Raindrops of grace can be found in the dark days of the turbulent storm. They are priceless jewels far richer than an abundance of raindrops in a spring shower. As the deeper mysteries of His kingdom are revealed, we find His love is not the neatly-wrapped package we may have imagined. We see it rage and roar as it is proven in the violent winds of life. He pursues us. All of us. We learn to endure because He never loses His grip. We learn to trust in His abiding presence, void of feeling. We learn to stop wrestling with Him and embrace the pain. And when the storm calms, we will look back and see His kindness and the inner abundance gained in the storm.

Father, I thank You in the dark storms of life, help me to see Your abundant kindness there.

Amen.

Sit quietly before God and silence your thoughts. Ask Him to reveal any sinful attitude you may have regarding your situation and ask Him to show you how He is using the storm in your life to draw you closer to Him. What may He be trying to teach you? What do you need to surrender at His feet? Journal your thoughts and then write down the raindrops of grace you are thankful for.

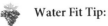 **Water Fit Tip:**

Measure the ounces in your favorite water bottle or glass and determine how many times you'll need to fill and drink from it each day to stay hydrated.

LEARNING TO FLOW

Marlene Dawson

"And when they arrest you, and deliver you up, do not be anxious beforehand about what you are to say, but say whatever is given you in that hour; for it is not you who speak, but it is the Holy Spirit."

~Mark 13:11 (NASB)

Learning to flow at the prompting of the Holy Spirit takes practice and patience. My youngest brother was preaching in China, and his female interpreter stood to his side, but out of his peripheral vision. Three times he made a statement, each with no response from her. He turned to see what happened, realizing she had fainted from the heat. No one moved to help her. He had EMT training, and his instinct said, *'Go to her,'* but the Holy Spirit stopped him. He did not know that in this culture a young man cannot touch a woman in public who is not his wife, but God knew. Helping her would have ruined my brother's credibility. However, his ministry partner lifted up and carried the young woman to the parsonage next door, where the ladies ministered to her needs. Since the partner was a grandfatherly type, it was not considered offensive for him to help. Another missionary who "happened" to be there stepped forward and finished interpreting for my brother.

God clearly tells us not to be anxious. The apostles knew they were instruments of God and could rely on the leading of Holy Spirit every time. We have the same direction to flow in the Holy Spirit. The thing we most often share is our testimony. People may argue doctrine, but they cannot argue when we say, "I used to be this, but God changed me, and now I am this." It is okay if we are not perfect in a given area, but we know God is changing us. The Holy Spirit gives us clear direction of what to do, or what not to do, when we listen to His leading. We do not need to worry about having the right words to speak when we believe God. No matter where we are speaking, or how stressful the situation, God will always lead us in the flow of His Spirit; that is a promise.

Lord, I sometimes get rushed, and forget your promises. Please help me to remember what You have already done in my life, so I can freely tell others. Thank You, Lord.

Amen.

Water Of The Holy Spirit

Remember a time when God up showed in your circumstances. How did the Holy Spirit lead you in a way that seemed odd? Did you listen or not? If you did, what came of it and who benefited from it besides you? If you did not listen, write a prayer of forgiveness releasing yourself today! Then make a decision to listen the next time!

_____
_____
_____
_____
_____
_____
_____
_____
_____
_____
_____
_____
_____
_____
_____
_____
_____
_____
_____
_____

Water Fit Tip:

Drinking from a straw helps you drink more water.

CARRIED BY GOD'S SUSTAINING GRACE

Lisa Danegelis

"He will yet fill your mouth with laughing, and your lips with rejoicing."

~Job 8:21 (NKJV)

My heart was flooded with a confusing flurry of excitement and dread. Our son's apprehension was visible. He was mixed race and, though we only knew him as our son, he had questions about his birth parents. We found them and they were meeting him for the first time. The decision to find them was heart wrenching and sacrificial in the most painful way only a parent would know. My world stood still as I worried that I wasn't mom enough for my own child. Motherly instincts told me to grab my son, run, and never look back.

What if they were the answer, the missing link to heal his troubled soul? What if they were his forever family, I thought as I watched them exchange a touch, a glance, and words? Their relationship began to grow and we allowed him to live with them to explore his place in that family. I have never found the words to describe the inadequacy and pain I felt during that time as his question marks faded.

In time his heart returned home and so did he. He fully embraced his forever family, and it was us. It was us! God gave us the strength to relinquish our son to what may have been a very different scenario.

Like Job, when God orchestrates a wilderness journey, you can be assured that, no matter how long, winding, and painful the path, you will be carried by His sustaining grace. When the clouds finally scatter and you shake the desert sand from your feet, a deep relief will settle in. You will look back upon the well-worn path, see God's promises fulfilled, and your mouth will resound with laughter!

Help me to trust that Your plans for my life will always end in laughter!

Amen.

WATER OF THE HOLY SPIRIT

Is the sound of your laughter foreign? Have struggles been consuming? Envision compartments in your soul as seasons of your life. Draw and name them. Mentally open doors of happiness from the past. Describe the feelings you had and remember your laughter. Imagine the doors from the future flinging open, brimming with new joy! Let the warmth flood you and settle deep into your soul. Thank God for the laughter you know is waiting for you!

 Water Fit Tip:

Want water that tastes better? Invest in a high-quality filter. This also helps eliminate the microorganisms that are camping-out in your tap water.

WATER THAT CLEANSES THE HEARTS

Kimberly Joy Krueger

Search me, O God, and know my heart! Try me and know my thoughts! And see if there be any grievous way in me and lead me in the way everlasting!
~Psalm 139:23-24 (ESV)

'The heart is deceitful above all things, and desperately wicked: who can know it?' Ouch. That was my first reaction during that Sunday sermon when I heard this verse. *'What a relief,'* was my second thought. Yes, to hear that the condition of my human heart was hopeless and that I would never be able to fully see its sin-sickness, was a relief. I know; that seems so contradictory! One single verse from the Bible finally told me what was wrong with me!

For years, I could not figure out why in the world I just couldn't get myself to do the right things. Worse yet, I couldn't even get my heart to want the right things. I wanted all the wrong things, all of the time and didn't know why. Now I knew why I struggled so—it was the condition of my heart! The preacher didn't just leave me with a terminal diagnosis; He went on to offer the cure. He passionately preached the good news that, in Christ, we receive a new heart. Wow! My old, sin-sick heart, gets a transplant? Well, sort of.

The new heart isn't exactly dropped in after the old, unreliable one is removed. A heart transplant is a traumatic procedure that involves cutting and breaking with blunt instruments like power saws! Thankfully, the Holy Spirit is much gentler than that. No, the new heart we receive is much more like a seed planted that needs "Son-light" and the Water of the Spirit to fully bloom and bear fruit. His Water goes to work on our hearts by way of cleansing conviction. The Holy Spirit sees what we cannot see—the dirt and debris that cause infection—and He is the only one who can wash it all away. The problem is that we are blinded by our dirt. I know I am.

Our dirt, or sin, blindness is why David prayed, *"Search me, O God, and know my heart…and lead me in the way everlasting!"* He knew that, left unto himself, he wouldn't see the danger and his heart would lead him astray. He needed a transplant and He knew the Holy Spirit was the Great Physician; and the only One equipped for the task. Can you relate?

Holy Spirit, search my heart for dirt and debris that is causing infection. Cleanse me of it all and lead me on a new path, with my new heart, where joy and freedom await me.

Amen.

WATER OF THE HOLY SPIRIT

After praying the prayer, sit quietly for a moment. What does the Holy Spirit want to cleanse you of today? Do you believe His motive is to prevent further pain and discomfort and instead, give you His best? Why or why not? If you are afraid to trust the Holy Spirit to search and cleanse your heart today, please write down what you think is holding you back.

 Water Fit Tip:

Carbonated sodas do not provide hydration; they actually dehydrate you. For every ounce of soda you drink, consume double the water first. (You'll find you'll crave less soda.)

BREAK THE CHAINS

Kathy Thorsen

"Peter said to them, "Repent, and be baptized every one of you in the name of Jesus Christ so that your sins may be forgiven; and you will receive the gift of the Holy Spirit. For the promise is for you, for your children, and for all who are far away, everyone whom the Lord our God calls to him."

Acts 2:38-39 (NRSVCE)

Do you ever hold onto unforgiveness, resentment or judgment towards yourself or others because it is easier than letting control of those thoughts go? My own marriage has been affected by the resentment I have held in my heart towards my husband because of occasions when I did not attempt to understand his point of view. For example, when we built our house I wanted to hire a particular builder but he insisted the job should be appointed to his friend. We now live in a beautiful home, but—at the time—I could not see the fortune at the end of the rainbow, as it was clouded by my desire to control a decision.

In *Matthew 18:21*, Peter asked how many times he needed to forgive. *"Jesus said to him, 'Not seven times, but seventy-seven times.'"* Even Peter wanted to maintain control over how much he needed to forgive. Thoughts of anger, resentment, and frustration not only poison our soul, but also affect the expression of our genes. The scientific study of epigenetics is starting to prove the link between the thoughts, emotions, and actions we choose to carry out and the healthy or detrimental expression of our genes. This foretelling of our actions affecting our "children's children" is represented throughout the Bible. (Science proves the Bible, again!) Prior to this passage, the people realized they had just crucified the "Divine Messiah," so they begged Peter to give instructions on what they should do.

God tells us to change our sinful thoughts and deeds so we may be washed by the Holy Spirit. He is calling us to break the chains of resentment, actively participate in forgiveness, and allow our hearts to be washed clean. God's promise applies to everyone who is willing to completely let go and faithfully travel down the river to freedom, from sin, through baptism and reconciliation. The gift of the Holy Spirit is not only available to the disciples of Jesus' era, but to all generations.

Thank You, God for Your generous gift of forgiveness for all my sins. I am heartedly sorry for holding resentment and unforgiveness towards myself and others. When I turn to You, grant me the courage so see what I need to let go, wash my transgressions, renew my heart, and create a clean spirit within me so that I may experience a peace that reaches far beyond my own being.

Amen.

Water Of The Holy Spirit

Who have you not forgiven, yourself, spouse, family member, friend, co-worker? What is God calling you to let go of first? Would you rather hang onto the feeling or would you rather experience the peace and freedom of letting it go?

_____

_____

_____

_____

_____

_____

_____

_____

_____

_____

_____

_____

_____

_____

_____

_____

_____

_____

_____

_____

Water Fit Tip:

You will be more likely to drink water if you have a bottle or glass of water in front of you or in the car with you at all times. Refill it each time its empty.

Perfect Timing

Kathy Carter

"You will joyfully draw water from the springs of salvation."

~Isaiah 12:3 (CSB)

I truly believe God places people, experiences, and items in your life at the perfect time. You do not realize it is perfect timing until you reflect days, months, even years later.

During the darkest days of my life, God placed a tiny devotional book in my hands. This was in 1985. I still have the book and deep memories of pouring myself into something that made me feel like someone. I had hope in this small book and a God I could not see, touch, or feel. At the time, I had no idea how powerful that was. I only knew the words on those pages gave me life again and—more than anything—love and acceptance. The words on those pages led me to make some tough decisions, start believing in something much greater than me, and believing in myself. That book literally saved my life. I didn't know the power of God back then. It was just a book full of truth that took a heavy burden off my shoulders.

Fast forward to 2017, when I decided at age fifty-five to officially accept the Lord as my savior publicly in baptism. God's heavenly water washed over me and made me new again. The experience changed my entire course in life, brought me closer to God, and gave me the courage to share my stories to help others.

In Isaiah 12:3, God tells us to reach out to Him and ask for His grace. Let the cool waters of salvation wash over you so you can feel new strength, courage, joy, and life. God will wait for you and His grace is everlasting. Our glorious God will meet all your needs. All you need to do is ask!

Dear God, thank You for Your everlasting grace and for Your patience in waiting for us to seek You. Wash over our sins and help us to reach for Your understanding and salvation. Forgive us when we choose other things over You, for we know You are the only strength we need. In Your name, Jesus Christ.

Amen.

Imagine a time when you felt at a crossroads or dead end in life. What methods did you use to get through this confusing time? Trusting that God has endless springs of salvation and grace for you, how do you envision yourself handling a similar situation next time? Do you believe it is never too late to accept God as your savior and why?

 Water Fit Tip:

Drink one eight-ounce glass of water when you wake, and then one before each meal. You will stay hydrated and eat less!

From The Cistern To The River

Tamara Fink

"God, You are my God; I shall seek You earnestly; My soul thirsts for You, my flesh yearns for You, In a dry and weary land where there is no water."

~Psalms 63:1 (NIV)

I remember the day so well. I wish I could forget it, actually. The news rattled me to the core. Another affair…how could this nightmare be happening again? My mind began to swirl to try to make sense of what I was hearing. How would I ever be able to sustain this pain again? The pain would wain only enough to allow the numbness to offer some relief. I would find myself sitting and staring out the window…I would engage my mind enough to hear the constant praise music I kept playing, hoping I would hear His voice. On my good days, I would dig into His Word passionately digging to find His heart for me. My flesh didn't desire the things of this world anymore. I desperately needed to be near Him, hear His voice and feel His love for me.

When the psalmist writes that he is earnestly seeking God, it's not a passive waiting. He is actively crying out for more of God. He is in search of and determined to discover the fullness of God's love. He knows that this world has nothing to offer.

It doesn't take much to see the weariness in our world. Turn on the news or any social media outlet and you'll see the exhaustion everywhere. People are physically exhausted, emotionally drained, their patience is gone, and their strength is fleeting. It's like the broken, dried up cisterns in Jesus' time. Those broken cisterns, or wells, were used as jails. Just as those dried up wells had no water to give and were only good for holding people captive, so are our longings when we try to quench our thirst with something other than God's love.

There is no replacement for the life-giving river of love that comes from Christ Jesus. He will quench every thirst.

Dear Heavenly Father, thank You for never running dry. Thank You for being my freedom and life source. Lord, help me to not look to empty wells to supply the desires of my heart. Remind me daily that You are all I need.

Amen.

How have you been trying to quench your thirst by going back to a dried up well? What cistern is holding you captive today? Ask Jesus to set you free today.

Water Fit Tip:

Dehydration symptoms include headaches, increased thirst, dry mouth, fatigue, decreased or dark urine, dry skin, or dizziness.

SUSTAINABLE ESSENTIALS FOR LIFE

Candice Moe

"Remember our history, friends, and be warned. All our ancestors were led by the providential Cloud and taken miraculously through the Sea. They went through the waters, in a baptism like ours, as Moses led them from enslaving death to Salvation Life. They all ate and drank identical food and drink, meals provided daily by God. They drank from the Rock, God's Fountain for them that stayed with them wherever they were. And the Rock was Christ. But just experiencing God's wonder and Grace didn't seem to mean much—most of them were defeated by temptation during the hard times in the desert, and God was not pleased."

~1 Corinthians 10:1-5 (MSG)

Water is essential for sustaining life. It's as fundamental to our bodies as the Holy Spirit is to our souls. If my recollection of a biology lesson serves me right, our hearts and brains are over seventy percent water while our lungs are comprised of an even more staggering percentage of over eighty percent. Our anatomy largely constitutes and is heavily dependent upon H2O. There exists a parallel in the spirit. For optimum functionality of spirit and soul, we must utilize Jesus' invitation to come and drink deeply from the river of Living Water that flows from the Father's heart and from the Lamb. (Revelation 22:1 MSG) Before I knew the Lord, my soul was so starved for hydration that it literally crumbled, but one glorious day I gave myself over, not only to Jesus, but also to His written Word. Life has since become an oasis of joy, peace, and fun.

The Bible says that husbands are to wash their wives in the cleansing water of Abba's Word. As believers in Christ, we are to be His bride; pure and holy, without spot or blemish. Jesus, your Bridegroom, desires to prepare you for betrothal. This subarrhation rests on intimacy. Relationship must mellow into fellowship. Maturity requires more than church attendance, it requires personal pursuit. Your betrothed longs to wash you and satisfy your thirsty soul. It is only by becoming a well yourself that you're able to thrive, soaring high above the pitfalls and demands of life. It is only when the Word becomes woven into the very essence of your soul that joy and peace resound, even before the circumstances change. We are called to live from the inside out. Peace, love, self-control, faith, patience . . . these grandeurs are contained within the pages of the Bible and can only be extracted by choice. We must choose to allow our Lord to cleanse us daily. We must choose intimacy. Jesus offers you Living Water that will reinvigorate your inner most being. *"This Water becomes a spring within you, welling up to eternal life ." (John 4:14 NIV)*

Father, forgive me if I have neglected quality time spent with You in Your Word. Ignite within me a passion for Fellowship and Your cleansing water. Help me rise beyond the cares of this world. I place my trust in You as You breathe upon the chapters I read each day.   *Amen.*

WATER OF THE HOLY SPIRIT

Just as water is essential to life, peace, joy and love are essential to spiritual life. Do peace, joy and love resound in your life—in spite of the circumstances? Do you live from the inside out? If yes, write a prayer of thanks to God for manifesting the Water of the Spirit in your life. If no, write your prayer of petition, asking Him to pour His Spirit upon you, teaching you to live from the inside out.

_____
_____
_____
_____
_____
_____
_____
_____
_____
_____
_____
_____
_____
_____
_____
_____
_____
_____
_____
_____

 Water Fit Tip:

Don't drink all your calories. Save calories and drink water, various teas (especially green tea), or black coffee. Skip the whip and chocolate in your coffee . . . save the calories for food.

A Word In Due Season

Susan Brozek

"For the Holy Spirit will teach you at that time what you should say."
~Luke 12:12 (NIV)

Have you ever found yourself in a position where you simply had no idea what to say? Or, on the contrary, have you been in situations where you have likely said too much? Or perhaps unkind words have shortsightedly poured forth, causing you to experience deep regret later on. This is why it is so important to be Holy Spirit-led when we choose our words. Words have the power to build others up or tear others down. Scripture tells us that *"the power of life and death is in the tongue."* Words essentially set the parameters for our lives. As an example, if we continue to speak out that we "won't amount to anything," we shouldn't be surprised when we experience exactly that. As children, those in authority over us possess the ability to help shape the course of our lives as well, with their own words. A parent who demeans and criticizes a child without any words of affirmation will affect that child's view of him or herself in untold ways. On the flip side, a parent who encourages a child, making it clear that he or she can become anything the child chooses to be, is setting the stage for healthy self-worth and a mentality of success.

The Bible also stresses the timing of our words to others. Proverbs tells us that *"well-timed words are like apples of gold in settings of silver."* It is so important to wait upon the Holy Spirit's timing when we are dealing with others. In my private practice, this is probably one of the key elements of my counsel to clients; speaking to them as the Holy Spirit directs me to...not just in content, but in timing. For instance, if something is said too soon, before a person has been made ready to receive it and its meaning for their life, it can be ineffective at best, and a stumbling block at worst. This obviously holds true for all of us regarding the relationships God has placed in our lives; we would do well to wait before opening our mouths to be sure that what we desire to say is what God would lead us to say, especially in instructional and advisory capacities.

Heavenly Father, render us sensitive to the impact and power of our words. Aid us, Holy Spirit, in seeking Your content and Your timing for those with whom we are privileged to be in relationship. Help us to remain patient and slow to speak if we feel a hesitancy from You in our interaction with someone.

Amen.

Think of some instances where you may have spoken hastily or without forethought. Have consequences or a breach in relationship resulted? Describe some examples of how you have built up and encouraged a hurting person by your words. How did you feel after that experience? What are some of the words and phrases that you remember being spoken over you the most as a child growing up? What do you think the results of those spoken words have been as you walk out your path in life?

Water Fit Tip:

Use an app on your smartphone to track your water intake.

LIVING WATER POURED OUT FOR US

Margaret Bentham-Moe

"David was thirsty for some water from his hometown, so he said, "Oh, if only I could have some water from that well by the gate in Bethlehem." So the Three Heroes[a] fought their way through the Philistine army and got some water from the well near the city gate in Bethlehem. They took it to David, but he refused to drink it. He poured it on the ground as an offering to the LORD. "

~2 Samuel 23:15-16 (ERV)

This account paints a vivid picture of the value placed on a certain type of water. It did not come from just any well, it was drawn from the well near the city gate in Bethlehem. David remembered the sweet taste and refreshing feeling he got from this water and longed to experience it again. At that time David was hiding in a cave in a place called Adullam (translated as "refuge" in the Hebrew language). David's longing for the water moved three heroic men, who had fought alongside him, to willingly risk their lives. It was no cakewalk to obtain the water as they had to break through the host of the Philistine army to get it. Having brought the water to David, he no longer saw it as simply water but the very lifeblood of these men. David felt that the only one worthy of receiving such a great sacrifice is God and so he poured out the water as an offering to the Lord.

It's interesting that the water that David longed to drink came from Bethlehem. In the Hebrew language Bethlehem means the House of Bread. Jesus, the Bread of Life, was born in Bethlehem and He is the only source of Living Water. *1 Samuel 2:22* says "Everyone that was in distress and everyone that was in debt and everyone that was discontented." Whatever we fit in those groupings it's only by drinking the Living Water of the Word of God that we will be set free. David never asked those three men to get him the water, yet—because of their love for him—they risked all to get it.

Jesus gave us all a command to reach the lost and He has equipped us with His Word. Do we love Him enough to lay down our own lives so that, as David poured out the water, we can present our lost souls before the Lord?

Our Father in Heaven, we are grateful for the gift of Your Son Jesus, increase in us the desire to lay down our lives for the sake of reaching those who are lost so that they too could come into a relationship with You through Jesus. We ask this in Jesus' mighty name.

Amen.

Water Of The Holy Spirit

What specific water do you crave in your life right now? What would life look like if you replaced your most-treasured possessions for a filling of God's Holy Spirit? Do you believe the Water of the Spirit is enough to quench that thirst? Write your prayer to God asking Him to quench your thirst now.

_____
_____
_____
_____
_____
_____
_____
_____
_____
_____
_____
_____
_____
_____
_____
_____
_____
_____
_____
_____
_____

Water Fit Tip:

Drinking sixteen ounces room temperature water mixed with several tablespoons fresh squeezed lemon juice or apple cider vinegar, with your probiotic, twenty minutes before eating breakfast, is a great way to start the day! It is a liver detoxifier, balances your PH, replenishes minerals, and much more.

THE LAW VERSUS GRACE

Susan Brozek

> "For the law was given through Moses; grace and truth came through Jesus Christ."
>
> ~John 1:17 (NIV)

Perfectionism.
Unrealistically high standards.
Over-achieving.
Legalism.

These are all characteristics that have defined many of us throughout our lives. In my case, it wasn't until fairly recently that I began to grasp the truth of what God's grace can do for a person bound up by man-made rules and regulations. Although there is definitely good that comes out of wanting to serve the Lord with excellence, a balance is important so that we don't become enslaved to self-effort. Who is it who gets to define what "perfect" is, anyway?

I believe our only true standard of perfection who has ever walked this earth is the Lord Jesus Christ Himself, the fullness of the Godhead bodily. And fortunately, because of His great love for us and His understanding of the limitations and challenges we face as we live out our lives in this fallen world, He also gives us grace! Not "cheap grace," not a "license to sin," but true grace that was purchased for us with His very life given up on the cross. Grace is unmerited favor, and there is absolutely nothing we can do . . . no performance, no accomplishment, no perfect achievement . . . to earn it.

Biblical scholars have debated which disciples were present at the cross when our Lord Jesus was crucified. Some believe that it was Peter, James, and John. In the original Biblical languages, names had very significant meanings: names of people often represented their character or notoriety. One meaning for the name Peter was "rock or stone." James (a derivative of Jacob), meant "to replace or supplant." John's name meant "grace."

If these three disciples were present at the cross, then Peter, the stone (upon which Moses wrote the original laws of the Ten Commandments), was replaced (James), by grace (John). At the cross, the law was replaced by grace!

Father God, we stand in awe of You and what You have done for us by sending Your only Son to die for us at the cross, and that He came not to abolish the Law, but to fulfill it, because You knew that we could not. Help us to fully grasp Your beautiful plan of redemption for us.   Amen.

WATER OF THE HOLY SPIRIT

Describe an area of your life in which you have difficulty showing grace to yourself, even knowing that God gives you His grace. How can you begin to work on receiving the grace of God more fully? In what ways do you feel your relationship with God would change and deepen if you truly walked in His grace? To help you get started, write about a time when you were shown grace and how it impacted you.

Water Fit Tip:

When you eat out, ask your server for a pitcher of water and plate of lemons to keep at your table.

HE'S A GOOD GOOD FATHER

Teresa Kliner

> "If you then, though you are evil, know how to give good gifts to your children, how much more will your Father in heaven give the Holy Spirit to those who ask him."
>
> ~Luke 11:13 (NIV)

When my kids were little, each night while I was putting them to bed my husband would come in and ask them if they wanted "fresh." What he was offering was to get them fresh, cold water for their sippy cups. This became a habit and—even when my husband didn't ask or wasn't home at bedtime—they would ask "Can you get me some fresh?"

I always looked at this as a procrastination tactic. The longer bedtime time took the better in their eyes. Plus, the more they drank before bed, the more times they were going to need to get up and go to the bathroom. I mean, I love my children but who wants to prolong bedtime? I was usually exhausted and ready to be done for the day. They didn't often drink much from their cups each night, so my logic was that they could just drink the leftovers from the night before. This whole routine annoyed me. I often tried to hurry up and pray and leave quickly, so they would hopefully forget to ask. It usually didn't work. However, my husband loved the "fresh" routine. He really thought this was something they needed and loved providing it for them.

I'm so thankful we have a good, good Father. One who isn't annoyed with us when we ask for a fresh outpouring of His love and blessings. One that believes we not only need his love and blessings, but deserve them. A father who loves providing for us. He is never content on handing out leftovers. His mercies are new every morning!

Heavenly Father, thank You for loving us so beautifully. Thank You that You care about us more than we could even imagine. Thank You for the gift of the Holy Spirit.

Amen.

Water Of The Holy Spirit

The Holy Spirit is described as our comforter, our refiner, our guide, and our power. How often do we ask for His help? How often do we seek his Spirit? It's a gift; we don't need to do anything but ask and He is ready to give.

Water Fit Tip:

Dilute sugary drinks with water and ice while transitioning to water only.

BE RAISED BY THE RISEN JESUS

Jane Guffy

> "But when he saw the wind, he was afraid, and beginning to sink he cried out, 'Lord, save me.'"
>
> ~ Matthew 14:30 (NIV)

We learn early that, without a floatation device, we sink in water. Gravity pulls us down. Our family loves boating and we've taken boater's safety classes. The U.S. Coast Guard checks boats for life jackets. When my kids were young, they took swimming lessons to learn to swim and respect the water. (My kids pre-date swimmies.) We taught them Rule #1: never dive into the water when it's an unknown.

Our time on Lake Michigan has taught us that winds can cause hidden undertows in the water. They pull you down and under, causing fatigue, which leads to drowning. Gravity, water, and winds are hidden forces would make anyone cry out, *'Save me!'*

Water is inviting! Gravity has pull. We can engage each of our five God-given senses to experience water: see, hear, touch, smell, and taste. We can't see gravity or wind, we can only witness and survive their strength and effects.

In physical water we sink. In spiritual water we are raised. Physical water is finite, recycled, re-used, filtered. Spiritual water is abundant, infinite, new, pure, and unfiltered. God created all water on Earth in the beginning. We cannot create new water.

God isn't making more water, no new water front property. God created the earth and everything in it. Everything needs physical water to live. God's people need gravity to hold us to Him and we need spiritual water to live forever, with Him.

Jesus is not a floatation device. Jesus isn't interested in basic water safety, treading water, or doing things man's way. Believers will be pushed by the energy of winds and held down by gravity. Keep your eyes on Jesus. Stay above the wrath of earthy forces and find Jesus in the call of salvation. Jesus saves! Living water!

Thank you, God, for answering my call of 'Save me!' when I fear the wind and get that sinking feeling in my life. You alone save.

Amen.

Water Of The Holy Spirit

When was your cry to be saved answered? What waves has that caused in your life? Do you face the winds head on or with your eyes on Jesus?

_____

_____

_____

_____

_____

_____

_____

_____

_____

_____

_____

_____

_____

_____

_____

_____

_____

_____

_____

_____

_____

 Water Fit Tip:

Drink at least half of your daily water requirement in the morning. This increases the odds that you will meet your daily goal and keeps you from having to use the bathroom at night.

FREE TO BE ME

Teresa Kliner

> "Now the Lord is the Spirit, and where the Spirit of the Lord is, there is freedom."
>
> ~2 Corinthians 3:17 (NIV)

I was challenged to ask God who He says I am. You see, I had been directed to the I AM statements and verses in the Bible many times. No matter how many times I read through them, they didn't help. Why? I had begun to believe that these things weren't true for me.

Was I good enough? Pretty enough? Thin enough? I never felt I was "Enough." I was comparing my perceived weaknesses with perceived strengths of others. I fully believed the I AM statements for everyone else but just not for me. Until one day God said *'What makes you so special? What sets you apart from everyone else in the world that my Word is true for them, but not for you?'*

If I couldn't believe these statements were true for me, I couldn't believe any of the Bible was true.

When I asked God who He said I am, there was so much freedom that came. He made me and He doesn't make mistakes. The Holy Spirit washed over me in such a powerful way. It was like a wave came and first knocked me over. It demolished the thoughts that I was any different than God's other children. Then came His refreshing water covering my whole being. He knew me. He loved me. I was free to be ME. He washed away the baggage of my past thoughts. Only His truth mattered.

We have all had an identity crisis before. Who am I really? If the enemy can keep us from knowing who we are, we are stuck. We are unable to tap into Christ's power through His promises. His promises are for His children. But we have to know and believe we are His children. He will bring freedom through His Holy Spirit. True freedom from the bondage we walk around with.

He will help us to see ourselves for who we really are. Whole and made new in Christ.

Lord, I pray that you would wash over each of us with your living water. Reveal to us our true identity in You. Bring healing and freedom into our lives.

Amen.

Water Of The Holy Spirit

It feels like the whole world is in an identity crisis. But the Word of the Lord gives us our identity. We just need to allow the Holy Spirit access over our lives and who we are. How can you allow God to shine his truth into your life? Do you believe that you can have freedom in Christ Jesus and the identity He has given you?

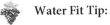 **Water Fit Tip:**

To help stay hydrated, eat water-rich foods like zucchini, cucumbers, watermelon, grapefruit, lettuce, and celery.

A Hopeful Energy

Tracy Hennes

"Oh! May the God of green hope fill you up with joy, fill you up with peace, so that your believing lives, filled with the life-giving energy of the Holy Spirit, will brim over with hope!"

~Romans 15:13 (MSG)

The dawn of a new day is often a sight to see. Sometimes there are shades of pink, purple, and orange, other times gray and yellow. The sunrise is even more impressive when the new light dances on the surface of water, wood, or glass. There is a calming peace about early morning. Whatever the colors may be, I greet each new day as an opportunity to be better than I was the day before. With an expectation for future good, negativity is washed away and the life-giving energy of the Holy Spirit can become so evident that it is difficult to contain. When an inspiring moment fills you to the brim, who do you want to share it with?

God gives us renewed hope and an expectation of better things to come. As the Holy Spirit fills us up to an overflowing level, we have an exhilarating opportunity to complete His will and share joy, peace, and hope with others. We do not need to question whether we are capable or ready. He doesn't call the qualified, He qualifies the called. We can approach each day and embrace it as another chance to renew our faith, in community together. God fills us each up in unique ways and gives us our own stories and messages. Let them flow over to others and be ready to receive and share in the messages from those around you as well.

Oh, God. How truly energizing You are! I thank You for the new, life-giving energy, hope, joy, and peace that You bring each day. I am sorry for the times that I have not allowed these to fill me up as I should. Help me to recognize and respond appropriately to others for whom the Holy Spirit is also brimming over. I'm welcoming You in, today and always. Let the overflow be for Your glory!

Amen.

WATER OF THE HOLY SPIRIT

There are some days when you may not be feeling like "brimming over with hope" or even being around other people. What do you think you could do about that in a God-honoring way? Sometimes, we become so weighed down in life that it's hard to recognize the uplifting. Use this journaling space to write about what fills you up with joy? Peace? How can you experience hope today?

 Water Fit Tip:

Infuse your water with herbs that enhance flavor, such as mint, or with citrus slices. Besides flavor, these ingredients provide a natural boost of energy.

Meet Our Authors

KIMBERLY JOY KRUEGER has overcome some of life's toughest struggles with beauty, dignity, and grace; her eyes always looking up and never looking back. She fell in love with running in 2014 and has since run more than ten 5Ks, half marathons, and full marathons. After being hit by a car in 2014, she ran a half marathon just eleven months later. Her favorite race to run is her race with God; and she runs it to win! As a third-generation entrepreneur, she has set her goals high and continues to reach higher, while helping women to see their true value and reach their God-given potential. Her mission is to empower women to live extraordinary lives and tell their stories. Through *The Fellowship of Extraordinary Women* (FEW) monthly meetings, FEW's Women's Leadership Course, and FEW International Publications, she is doing just that—by leaps and bounds. Kimberly says that her greatest accomplishment in life is being a wife, mother to twelve children, and "Noni" to five (perfect) grandchildren. Her closest friends will tell you that she is a mom to many and a friend to all. For fun, she transforms into a "Biker Chic," and rides alongside her husband, Scott, on her Harley-Davidson® Road King. Visit ***www.kimberlyjoykrueger.com*** for more information.

From a very young age, **TAMARA FINK** has always wanted to help people. She began pursuing her dream by getting her Bachelor's of Science in Psychology and, upon completion of college, she obtained a job in social services helping women become self-sufficient financially. Currently, she is a small business owner who helps people find health through nutrition. Through her adult years, she has weathered many storms, yet her heart's desire is still to help others become whole in every aspect of their lives; bodies, souls, and spirits. By sharing her journey, she believes others can find their ways to wholeness. Tamara passionately believes that every part of our being must be healthy, in order to lead a full and abundant life. Just like her name means, "Palm Tree," she longs to come alongside women and show them the gift of bending, not breaking, and rising up to be stronger than ever, by being deeply rooted in the word of God. You can often find her reading, hiking, or enjoying time with her family. Please visit: *tamarafink.com* to follow her latest happenings.

SUSAN BROZEK, M.S.W., L.C.S.W., is the Director and Founder of Healing Word Psychotherapy Services LLC. (*www.healing-word.com*), and her heart and call is to help hurting people. She has been a licensed clinical Christian psychotherapist for nearly twenty years. Susan has spoken at many conferences state-wide. She also hosted a weekly radio program called *Healing of the Mind*. She and her husband Jeff are the published authors of *HEALING WORDS: 30 Devotional Word Studies for Emotional and Spiritual Healing* (©2005). Susan and Jeff enjoy traveling, boating, kayaking, and spending time with their Golden Retrievers. They live in Mequon, Wisconsin with frequent trips to Door County, Wisconsin.

KATHY CARTER has been a fitness professional since college. Outside of being active with her family, competing in running events, and teaching exercise classes at her favorite clubs, you will find her spreading natural health and wellness through her Zija business. Whether a competition or just for fun, Kathy always gives it her all. Once she realized she had neglected to feed and strengthen the most important part of her body, her soul, it became very important for her to share her testimony with others. Her mission is to help other women become *Holy, Whole, and Fit*. Visit **kathycarter.org** to learn more.

LISA DANEGELIS and her family live in the beautiful state of Wisconsin. She attended a culinary program where she fell in love with and married her instructor thirty-one years ago. Together, they own the prestigious Lee John's Catering. She is also a busy mom of five adopted children and a survivor of wrongly prescribed psychiatric drugs. She has her own YouTube channel and Facebook group to support others on this harrowing journey. In time, she hopes to use her home as a safe haven for those in need. Lisa enjoys gardening, yoga, and writing. You may contact her at: *Bakingfever@yahoo.com*.

MARLENE DAWSON is a #1 bestselling author and retired special education paraprofessional. Marlene has a deep desire for women to know God's healing love, as she knows what courage it takes to face life's painful circumstances. She is part of a ministry team that helps women move forward from difficult situations. Marlene is a conference speaker who teaches on faith, healing, and prayer. Marlene and her husband, Jim, live in Wisconsin, have four children, and look forward to grandbaby number eight on the way. Marlene enjoys grandparenting, family times, traveling, and writing. To contact Marlene, please visit: *marlenedawson.com*.

REBECCA GRAMBORT is a speaker, coach, and bestselling author with FEW International Publications. She is also a marathoner and enjoys challenging herself by training year-round for long distance races. Her other interests include down-hill and cross-country skiing; kayaking and playing her piano. She resides in Merrill, Wisconsin and is a wife to her devoted husband and a proud mother of four. This devotional work is her third publication with FEW and her other contributions may be found in FEW's "Effect" Series books, *The Ah-Ha Effect* and *The Miracle Effect*. Visit **www.mahmonline.com** for more information

JANE GUFFY is a small business entrepreneur, mother of five, Gigi of four (so far) and has been involved in ministries and organizations aimed at impacting women through fellowship. After years of involvement on school boards, family advocacy organizations, and families in need, Jane has invested the last few years and her resources into creating relationships among women through faith. She believes strongly in building bonds between women (as they journey through the seasons of life) and collaborating, so each woman's life is meaningful and noteworthy. Jane and her husband, Doug, love building family memories into the next generation.

#1 Bestselling author, TRACY HENNES, has eighteen years of experience as a speech-language pathologist and a firm belief in the power of communication. As a small business owner, she combines faith, values, and a passion for wellness, with her drive and desire to serve others. Tracy is a certified yoga instructor who devotes time daily to reading and reflecting on God's Word, drawing upon that in daily activities, leading others through inspirational book studies, and yoga. Tracy enjoys quality time with her three children, husband, and their many pets in Washington County, Wisconsin. Find her hiking, cooking, and working out in fun t-shirts! Please visit **www.tracyhennes.com** for more information.

TERESA KLINER has a love for people and a passion to see them whole and free in Christ. Along with this and her strong faith in God, she has a desire to help others find health; physically, emotionally, and spiritually. Her journey with her own health in these areas has given her insight that she is excited to share with others. Teresa enjoys getting outside to run any chance she can and she loves spending family time with her husband and four children. You can follow her on her journey by subscribing to her blog at *teresakliner.wixsites.com/website*.

CANDICE MOE is a young woman with a passion for the Person, the Presence and the unchanging Word of God. She emphasizes the great importance of continuously reading the Bible and the Holy Spirit regularly opens up the scriptures and their mysteries to her (Proverbs 25:2). Without a doubt, the Father's Love is what changed her life and wonderfully turned her heart Heavenward. Born on the beautiful Caribbean island of Trinidad, Candice is the first of her parent's five children and has a love for travel and adventure. She blogs at *candicemoethekingsdaughter.wordpress.com* and on "Candice Moe Ministries" on Facebook.

MARGARET BENTHAM-MOE is a Christian, wife to the love of her life, Garnet, and a mother to her five beautiful gifts: Candice, Cherisse, Chenelle, Chad, and Chakeil. She's a firm believer in the absolute truth of the Bible as the inerrant word of the True and Living God. Her greatest desire is to see people come to the realization of our Heavenly Father's love for His children; Jesus' love and His priceless gift purchased on the Cross of Calvary; the power of His Blood and the Person of the Holy Spirit to enable us to fulfill destiny. Margaret blogs at *theinerrantwordofofgod.wordpress.com*.

LUANNE NELSON is a motivational speaker, certified health coach, and published author. As a coach, she encourages men and women to learn new skills to attain healthier lifestyles. Luanne understands the importance of nurturing body, soul, and spirit to achieve optimal fitness. Heeding this awareness, she and her husband, David, both are certified health coaches and ordained ministers. Together, they work street ministries, spreading God's Word of Salvation while encouraging community participation in the Works of Mercy. Luanne and her husband reside in Milwaukee, Wisconsin. She enjoys photography, gardening, and antiquing. Visit *www.LuanneNelson.com* for more information.

DANELLE SKINNER loves her family tremendously. They inspire her to become her best. She says, "I am very much a work-in-progress". She studies Jesus and His ways in the Bible to become kinder, more patient, and more love-focused. It is there Jesus helps her on her journey to become a better version of herself. Changing her little by little from the inside out. She wants to encourage you to dig into His word, unpacking what it means for your life today, not just for eternity in Heaven. It will put life into your mind, body and soul. Glory to Him!

KATHY THORSEN inspires many with God's message through music ministry. As a former chemistry teacher and current student in the Functional Medicine Health Coaching Academy, she follows her passion for learning and teaching about God's creation. Kathy's new business, A Plus Health, LLC., allows her to empower others to achieve their wellness goals through self-reflection of lifestyle choices. Kathy enjoys supporting her three children and their interests, as well as singing, playing the piano, practicing yoga, and experimenting in the kitchen. Kathy and her husband live in Wisconsin and they enjoy traveling the world. Visit: *www.a-plushealth.com* for more information.

ARE YOU READY TO TELL YOUR EXTRAORDINARY STORY?

Become a FEW International Publications Author
Write your own story with FEW,
Or request information about contributing to a collaborative book in one of our collections:
"The Effect Series" (collections of women's true short stories)
"A FEW Words" (collaborative devotional series)

Email: Kimberly@TheFewWomen.com for more information.

Extraordinary Women; Extraordinary Stories
http://kimberlyjoykrueger.com/few.php

An Invitation to Become
Holy, Whole, and Fit in Jesus Christ

We believe every woman desires to be *Holy, Whole, and Fit* in spirit, soul, and body.

The good news of the Gospel is that we can be! The promise for those who have been saved by grace through faith in Jesus Christ is that *"he who began a good work in you will carry it on to completion."*

Are you assured of your salvation in Jesus Christ? If so, you can also be assured that He will finish what He started in you. If not, you can receive that assurance today by receiving His free gift of salvation. We invite you to pray this prayer today and begin your journey to becoming *Holy, Whole, and Fit*.

Father, I believe that your Son, Jesus, lived on this earth to ultimately die for me. I know I've sinned; I've missed the mark many times and I cannot save myself. I know that no amount of good deeds can wash me clean – but You can!

Today, I choose to place my trust in the price you paid on the cross. I now turn from my sin and my own ways and I turn toward You. Your death and resurrection were enough to set me free and to make me Holy, Whole, and Fit for your coming!

Thank You for dying for me and giving me the gift of eternal life. Now, I ask your Holy Spirit to fill me with boldness and to guide me to live for You.

Amen.

Made in the USA
San Bernardino, CA
17 April 2018